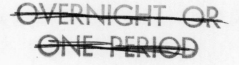

Recollections
of a
Georgia Loyalist

The Reprint Company
Spartanburg, South Carolina

The Reprint Company
Post Office Box 5401
Spartanburg, South Carolina 29301

Reprinted: 1972
ISBN 0-87152-083-4
Library of Congress Catalog Card Number: 76-187388

Manufactured in the United States of America on long-life paper.

Recollections

OF A

Georgia Loyalist

ELIZABETH LICHTENSTEIN JOHNSTON
in early life

Recollections

OF A

Georgia Loyalist

BY

ELIZABETH LICHTENSTEIN JOHNSTON
Written in 1836

EDITED BY

REV. ARTHUR WENTWORTH EATON, B.A.

Author of "The Church of England in Nova Scotia and the Tory Clergy of the Revolution," "Acadian Legends and Lyrics," "The Olivestob Hamiltons," etc., etc.

THE DE LA MORE PRESS

52 High Holborn . . . . London

New York . . M. F. MANSFIELD & CO.

PREFACE

ONE of the most interesting chapters of American history, the chapter that fairly describes the Loyalists, or Royalists, of the Revolution, and adequately tells their subsequent fate, for the most part remains yet to be written. It is commonly estimated that when the North American colonies had finally become the United States, the population of the country was less by a hundred thousand than before the war began. To England, Upper Canada, the West India Islands, and last, but by no means least, the fertile Province of Nova Scotia, the proud, unflinching, sorrowing Tories flocked. To the latter Province, which then included the sister Province of New Brunswick, certainly fully thirty thousand went, many with Howe's fleet at the evacuation of Boston, far more from New York, when the proclamation of independence was finally made. Of the many interesting facts of Nova Scotia history, a few, such as

Preface

the tragical expulsion of the Acadians, are comparatively well known, but the hardly less tragical story of the migration of the Loyalists to Nova Scotia, and the subsequent changes in their eventful lives, is one that at last is coming to have its proper interest for the American mind.

When Howe's fleet reached Halifax in 1776, the little town founded by Cornwallis and his English emigrants only in 1749, was taxed beyond its utmost limits to provide food and the most temporary shelter for so large a crowd. When Shelburne and the adjacent country in the more southerly part of the Province was reached by the New York people in 1784, for these cultivated men and women, many of them from the most luxurious American homes, there were at first only tents and rude cabins for shelter, and the scantiest provision for the other needs of life. If the actual hardships of even a few of these Loyalist families were ever completely told, the narrative would lack few points of interest of the saddest romance.

Of many of the Nova Scotia Loyalists the names alone are sufficient to awaken deep interest in the whole story of the migration.

6

Preface

We have, for example, the name of the second Mather Byles, rector of Christ Church, Boston, who with his family fled to Halifax, and was proscribed and banished in 1778. We have Jacob Bailey, the "Frontier Missionary," whose extraordinary sufferings from the patriots in Maine, and whose final settlement in the rectorship of St. Luke's Church, Annapolis, Nova Scotia, are well-known facts. We have Daniel, John Murray, and Jonathan Bliss, of Massachusetts, who long occupied distinguished positions in the judiciary of New Brunswick. We have Gen. Timothy Ruggles, of Hardwick, President of the Congress of Nine Colonies at New York, in 1765; Dr. John Halliburton, of Rhode Island (father of Sir Brenton Halliburton, eighth Chief Justice of Nova Scotia); the Hon. Rev. Jonathan Odell, of New Jersey, one of the poets of the Revolution; the Hon. Thomas Barclay of New York, who in 1799 succeeded Sir John Temple, Bart., as England's Consul-General to the United States; and among other prominent public men, Sir John Wentworth, Governor of New Hampshire, who in 1792 became Governor of Nova Scotia and in 1795 was created a baronet; and Dr.

Preface

Charles Inglis, of New York, who in 1787 became the first Colonial Bishop of the British Empire.

Among the many hundreds of names in Sabine's "Loyalists," the catalogue of which carries one completely through the alphabet, are to be found the names of Lewis and Andrew Johnston. Of Lewis Johnston, "residence unknown," it is said that he was banished and attainted, and his estate confiscated, and that in 1794 he represented to the British Government, by his attorney, John Irvine, that at the time of his banishment several large debts were due him in America, which he had not been able to recover. Of Andrew Johnston, captain in the Florida Rangers, it is merely said that he was killed in the attack on Augusta, Ga., in 1780. In the names of these men, who were father and son, there is nothing to suggest unusual interest, nor does Sabine apparently know more about them than he has here told, but we venture to believe that the following pages of reminiscence by a member of the distinguished Georgia family to which they belonged, will not by any means be found wanting, at least in variety of incident and in

Preface

strong human feeling.   The " Recollections"
were written in 1836, by Mrs. William Martin Johnston, then aged seventy-two, a woman
of strong character, clear intellect, and deep
religious feeling, and with a life behind her
unusually full of vicissitude and change.   As
the reminiscences show, she was born and
married in Georgia, at the time of the war
was obliged to flee to Florida, thence went
to Scotland, next settled in the West Indies,
and at last, by a singular fate, became, as she
remained till her death, a resident of Nova
Scotia.   In that Province and in other parts
of Canada her descendants have held, and
still hold, positions of the highest social and
political importance.   That these " Recollections" are of very wide historical or even
biographical interest, no one could possibly
claim; but the writer, who belonged to an
important colonial family, lived through an
exciting period of American history, bore her
share in the heavy personal misfortunes of
the political party to which she and her family belonged, spent her subsequent life in two
separate British colonies, took many long
voyages in uncomfortable sailing vessels on
stormy seas, and left descendants who have

9

Preface

always stood high in the public esteem. Thus her fortunes cannot fail to be interesting to any who have followed sympathetically the fate of the Loyalists of the Revolution.

One of the sons of the writer of these reminiscences, Judge James William Johnston, born in Jamaica in 1792, was successively Solicitor-General, Attorney-General, Judge in Equity, and Governor-elect of Nova Scotia. Her two sons-in-law were Judge Thomas Ritchie of Annapolis, First Justice in the Court of Common Pleas, and the Hon. William Bruce Almon, M.D., M.L.C., a Halifax physician of the highest professional and social standing. Her grandsons, among others, were the Hon. John William Ritchie, Solicitor-General and Judge in Equity of the Supreme Court; Sir William Johnston Ritchie, Judge of the Supreme Court of Nova Scotia, Chief Justice of New Brunswick, Judge of the Supreme Court of Canada, and Chief Justice of Canada; Hon. Joseph Norman Ritchie, Judge of the Supreme Court of Nova Scotia; Rev. James J. Ritchie, Rector of St. Luke's Church, Annapolis; Hon. William Johnston Almon, M.D., a distinguished physician of Halifax, and a member

Preface

of the Senate of Canada; Andrew Belcher
Almon, barrister (residing at Newport, R. I.);
and the Rev. Foster H. Almon, a clergyman
of Halifax, the last three of whom are also
great-grandsons of the second, and great-
great-grandsons of the first, Dr. Mather Byles.

The history of the Johnstons of Georgia,
Jamaica, and Nova Scotia, is briefly this.
About 1750, Dr. Lewis Johnston, surgeon
in the Royal Navy, on Her Majesty's ship
Centurion, a young Scotchman of excellent
family, the son of Dr. James Johnston, R. N.,
and his wife, Jane Nesbitt, married in St.
Kitts, in the West Indies, and then settled
as a physician in Savannah, Ga. There,
until the war broke out, he was in the best
city practice, owning also, a little out of the
town, a plantation called "Annandale," after
the famous estate of the Johnstones in Scotland. For a number of years he occupied the
important position of Treasurer of the Province and President of His Majesty's Council,
and so high did he stand in the public estimation that for years after he was obliged to
leave Savannah he was consulted in matters
of importance by his old patients and friends
in the Province where he had so long honor-

ably lived. In 1782, for his loyalty to the Crown, he was compelled to leave Georgia for Florida, and until East Florida was ceded to the Spaniards in 1784, he lived at St. Augustine. When it was necessary for him to leave Florida, the British Government gave him a transport to take him to any part of His Majesty's dominions he wished, and he naturally chose to return to Scotland, his native land. The remainder of his life he spent in Edinburgh, where he worshipped at the Greyfriars' Church, and where he died, October 9, 1796, at the age of seventy-two, his remains being interred in the old cemetery at the foot of the Calton Hill.

Dr. Johnston's wife, Laleah Peyton, who before her marriage was the *protégée* of her uncle, William Martin, a planter in St. Kitts, bore her husband, it is said, some twenty children, two sons of whom were William Martin Johnston, M. D., and the Andrew Johnston of Sabine's "Loyalists," both captains on the Tory side in the war. In the service of their King were also enlisted two younger sons of the family, Alexander and John. Of the sisters there were Elizabeth, wife of Dr. Irwin of Savannah; Laleah,

Preface

Sarah, Nancy, and Rachel. The author of these "Recollections," as we have seen, was the wife of Captain William Martin Johnston, and in 1848, when she was eighty-four years old, she gave her grandson, the Hon. William Johnston Almon, M.D., in writing, the following additional statement of the part taken by her husband and his brothers in the Revolution. Mrs. Johnston writes:

"Dr. Lewis Johnston had two sons captains in the army: William Martin Johnston, captain in the New York Volunteers, afterward numbered the Third American Regiment, who saw much active service and proved himself a brave officer, and Captain Andrew Johnston, who belonged to the King's Rangers, well known as Colonel Brown's Corps. In 1780, when his regiment was shut up by the enemy in the city of Augusta, a hundred and thirty miles from Savannah, and the men were in want of provisions, Colonel Brown asked who would venture on a sortie, to bring in provisions. Andrew Johnston instantly said he would go, provided he might choose his men. He was so beloved that all his men would have gone had he wished. He took as many as he wanted, went off, achieved most gallantly his object, but in returning, sad to relate, received a shot in the back and was killed. He was much lamented, for he was not only a brave officer but was most amiable in his disposition and exemplary in his character.

"His excellent father was sitting in Council with the Governor, Sir James Wright, when a countryman was shown in, just arrived from Augusta. On asking him the news from there he said, 'Not much, only there had been a *scrimmage.*' Being asked if any lives were lost, he answered, 'Only Captain Johnston's.' We may draw a veil over the father's feelings; of course, he retired instantly. I will relate one more circumstance to show the heroism of the mother, who was living at the time of the siege of Savannah, though dead at the time of her son Andrew's death. The siege of Savannah in 1779 was made by the combined forces of French and Americans with about 10,000 men, when the British force was not more than 1,800 men. Colonel Maitland with 500 men had previously gone on an expedition on the Carolina side, and it was feared he would not be able to effect a junction with

Preface

the troops in Savannah. The two Captain Johnstons were within the lines, at each extremity. They had two younger brothers, Alexander and John—the latter aged nearly fifteen and the former nearly sixteen—who wished much to join their brothers, but Mrs. Johnston would not hear of it, and told her elder sons, who also wished it, not to say a word more; she had risked two sons already and she would not have the others leave her on any account. All her family but myself had gone for safety from the balls and shells thrown into the town, to an island opposite the town, and in the barn in which our family were, there were fifty-eight women and children. All had dear friends in the lines. I remained with Mrs. Johnston and her two lads, as I was engaged to her oldest son and wished to stay to see him as often as I could. One morning Captain William M. Johnston came up in haste to tell his mother to set out immediately to the wharf and get a friend there to get us a boat, to cross without loss of time to the island, as the enemy were going to open a heavy cannonade upon the town. We set off without delay, and just as we turned the first corner of the street their batteries were opened, and the balls whizzed about our ears at an awful rate; never can I forget it. The firing was kept up fiercely for a good while, and at last Mrs. Johnston stopped in the middle of the street, and said: ' My boys, I was about to disgrace you; go and join your brothers'; which they did. Alex went to his brother William, who was quick-tempered and had great veneration for his mother. William thought the boy had run away without her leave, and accordingly received him, before he could explain, with a slap on the face for his disobedience. When the matter was explained, however, William kept the boy through the siege, and later he became a lieutenant in the New York Volunteers. John (who was the father of Judge Johnston of Trinidad) went to his brother Andrew, who was very good-natured and more patient in hearing his story, and remained with him and afterward became a merchant.

"During the siege Colonel Maitland made his way to us, and raised the spirits of the people very much, and on the 9th of October, 1779, at break of day, the enemy attacked the city with small arms. Previously the shells and cannon balls had done little damage, and the shot going over our men's heads, gave us far less fear than the appalling sound of the small arms. We all had near and dear connections in the line. Mrs. Johnston had her good old husband, and she sat in silence without uttering a word; I had my father and another very dear to me, who six weeks later became my husband. At 10 o'clock we got word that the enemy were beaten off, and that our friends were all safe, and O what thanksgiving, what joy we felt at so unexpected a deliverance! The French fought gallantly, too. We soon made war on the poultry and animals, and had a good dinner prepared for our friends. In all the American accounts they take little notice of our memorable siege. With the American army was the Polish Count Pulaski, and he was killed that morning.

"Your grandfather, my husband, after the war was over was on half pay, and in 1784–5 prosecuted his medical studies in Edinburgh, these having been interrupted by the war. Finally he settled and was for many years an eminent and successful Doctor of Medicine in Kingston, in the Island of Jamaica. I

Preface

have given you, dear William, a rather
lengthy detail, from which you may extract
whatever you like for publication. As you
know, I was present through the siege and
myself saw very nearly everything I have
here described.

"Your affectionate grandmother,

"E. JOHNSTON."

"HALIFAX, *July* 12, 1848."

"It will be observed that the war which had opened in
Massachusetts was steadily drifting southward. Great
campaigns had been fought in what are known as the Middle States, which continued to be the theatre of operations
for several years. In the extreme South, matters were in
a deplorable condition. Tories were numerous, and in
many places civil war reigned. The patriots were so few
in numbers that the enemy prepared a careful campaign for
the capture of Savannah and the conquest of Georgia.
Five thousand additional troops were to be landed at
Charleston, and a strong force of Indians was to be brought
from Florida and Alabama to assail the frontier settlements,
while the commandant at Detroit was to send others to
join them from the Northwest.

"General Prevost, who was in command of a mingled
force of regulars, Tories, and Indians in East Florida,
sent two expeditions in the autumn of the year 1778 from
St. Augustine, Florida. They committed many outrages
and brought away an enormous amount of plunder. In
the latter part of November, Clinton despatched Lieuten-
ant-Colonel Campbell, with two thousand troops, to invade
Georgia. The troops went by the sea and landed at Sa-

Preface

vannah on the morning of December 29th. The patriot general, Robert Howe, of North Carolina, with less than a thousand dispirited men, hurried up from Sunbury, and three miles below Savannah, at Brewton's Hill, fought a battle with a much superior force, and was badly defeated. In the flight through rice-fields and streams, a hundred patriots were drowned and four hundred made prisoners. The others who succeeded in escaping took refuge in South Carolina, while the enemy occupied Savannah."—Ellis' "History of the United States," vol. ii., pp. 524–5.

"A fleet sailed from New York via Sandy Hook on the 8th of November, 1778, for Savannah. The troops were under the command of Colonel Campbell, of the 71st Regt., and the New York Volunteers were of the expedition. On the 27th of November the fleet, which had been detained by storms, at length sailed. On the 24th of December we sailed into Savannah River, and on the 29th the troops disembarked, and were carried in flat boats and landed not far from the city. The enemy, who numbered about 800 men, did not make a long stand. Our loss was 20 killed and wounded. The rebel loss was 80 killed and wounded, and 400 prisoners. On the 31st we started for the city and took possession of Advocate Farley's house, in which we found a fine library."—Extract from the letter of a German officer, dated Savannah, January 16, 1779, kept in Mrs. Johnston's possession.

"The next year an attempt was made by the Americans, assisted by the French fleet, to capture Savannah, but it failed. In this attack Pulaski lost his life. After a regular siege, a British fleet and army took Charleston in May, 1780."—Eggleston's "History of the United States," p. 184.

"Early in 1782 the British Parliament, perceiving the futility of attempts hitherto to subdue the Americans, now

Preface

began to listen to the voice of reason and humanity, and steps were taken toward the establishment of peace between the United States and Great Britain, upon the basis of the independence of the former. On the fourth of March the House of Commons passed a resolution in favor of peace, and active hostilities ceased. Preparations were now made for the evacuation of Savannah, and on the eleventh of July the British army evacuated it, after an occupation of three years and a half. Wayne, in consideration of the services of Colonel James Jackson, appointed him to ' receive the keys of Savannah from a committee of British officers.' He performed the service with dignity, and on the same day the American army entered Savannah, when royal power ceased in Georgia forever. . . .

''Governor Martin called a special meeting of the Legislature in Savannah about three weeks after the evacuation. They assembled in the house of General McIntosh. . . . The session was short, but marked by decision and energy. On the first Monday in January following, the constitutional session commenced at the same place. Every branch of the new government was speedily organized, and the free and independent State of Georgia began its career."—Lossing's ''Field Book of the Revolution," vol. iix., p. 741.

In a note Lossing says:

"Between the 12th and 25th of July (1782), seven thousand persons, according to British accounts, left Savannah, consisting of 1,200 British regulars and Loyalists, 500 women and children, 300 Indians, and 5,000 negroes. Governor Wright and some of the civil and military officers went to Charleston, General Clarke, and part of the British regulars to New York, Colonel Brown's rangers and the Indians to St. Augustine, and the remainder under convoy of the *Zebra* frigate, the *Vulture*

Preface

sloop-of-war, and other armed vessels, to the West Indies. It is estimated that nearly seven-eighths of the slaves in Georgia were carried off now and on previous occasions, by the British."

The last battle for independence in Georgia was fought between Colonel Jackson and some British troops on Skidaway Island, below Savannah, on the 25th of July, 1782.

INTRODUCTION

BY

HON. WILLIAM JOHNSTON ALMON, M.D.
Senator of the Dominion of Canada

THE following "Recollections" were written by my grandmother, Mrs. Johnston, from memory, for the information of her grandchildren. She was, as she states, the only daughter of John Lichtenstein (anglicized Lightenstone), who was born in Cronstadt, near St. Petersburg, Russia, where his father had settled and where the latter conducted an academy for the education of youth.

Vitus Bering, a native of Denmark, and an admiral in the Russian navy under Peter the Great, from whom the Bering Straits received their name (though in reality he never visited them, as the cape he supposed to be the northeast point of Asia is now proved to

Introduction

be a cape far south of the real northeast cape) was a connection of the family. Captain John Lichtenstein, the father of the author of this journal, had in his possession a stone adze fastened to a wooden handle with reindeer thongs, which Bering had obtained in Kamschatka and had given to his (Lichtenstein's) father. This, Captain Lichtenstein brought to Annapolis Royal after the American War, and it is now in the Provincial Museum at Halifax, incorrectly labeled " Stone implement from the West India Islands, presented by Judge Norman Ritchie."

Captain Lichtenstein died at Annapolis Royal and was interred in the graveyard, where a stone to his memory exists. He emigrated from Russia to Georgia, where he obtained a portion of land in the Island of Skidaway—grants of which, bearing the dates of George II., are in my possession.

Mrs. Johnston, the daughter of Captain Lichtenstein, was married in Savannah, November 21, 1779, at the early age of fifteen, to Captain William Martin Johnston, M.D., born in Savannah, May 24, 1754, a captain in the New York Volunteers or Third Loyal

HON. WILLIAM JOHNSTON ALMON, M.D.
Senator of the Dominion of Canada

Introduction

American Regiment. Captain Johnston, at the commencement of the troubles between the revolting colonies and the mother country, was studying medicine in Philadelphia as a private pupil of Dr. Rush, one of the signers of the Declaration of Independence.[1]

I have in my possession a series of letters written by Captain Johnston's father to him, which in my opinion in elegance of diction equal those of Chesterfield to his son, while in the morality of the advice they give they are far superior. Among other things he finds fault with him for a serious disturbance he had had with a night watchman. Upon asking my grandmother (Mrs. Johnston) what this trouble was, she said that gentlemen in those days usually carried small swords in full dress, and that having what our American friends would call "a little difficulty" with the custodian of the night, he drew his sword on him. I, being a small boy at the time, inquired, "Did he run him through, grandmother?" She replied, "No,

[1] Dr. Johnston died at Kingston, Jamaica, December 9, 1807; his wife died at Halifax, Nova Scotia, "in full assurance of salvation through Christ," September 24, 1848.

dear, he only pricked him; but they made a great fuss about it."

To those who remember the accounts of the exploits of the "Mohawks" at night in the streets of London, as related in the pages of the *Spectator*, it will be known that such encounters were not uncommon in the reign of Queen Anne.

It may not be out of place here to transcribe a letter which Dr. Lewis Johnston wrote his son in reference to this affair:

"SAVANNAH, *Nov.* 19, 1774.

"DEAR BILLY: I rec'd yours of the 22d ult. by Captain Bunner, and have a full reliance on the promise you make me of making amends by your future conduct for your past indiscretions, which will be the best, and indeed only method of atonement. I am glad to find by Dr. Rush's letter that your behavior since that unhappy affair with the watchman has been unexceptional. I wish you had put it in his power to have added that your application to your studies had been diligent and constant, as that would have made me easy and happy. You owe much to that gentleman for the generous care he has taken of you. By every letter I receive from him I am more convinced of the friendship he has for you, and it should be your

Introduction

care to cherish it by every means in your power; this you are bound to do from a proper sense of gratitude, and from regard for your own interest. He certainly can and will be of much service to you in the prosecution of your studies if you are not much wanting in your own endeavor to profit by the opportunities you now enjoy."

To this advice I may add that which he gave his son on the threatened outbreak of the rebellion, which was then looming in the near future:

"SAVANNAH, GA., *Aug.* 20, 1774.
"DEAR BILLY:
". . . There is one thing which I think it my duty to caution you against, that is, the taking any part in the unhappy political disputes which I doubt not run very high in Philadelphia; these are matters you have no business with, and of which you cannot be supposed to be a competent judge. This consideration alone should induce you to be silent on the subject, but there is a prudential one which ought to have the greatest weight with you in your present situation, which is that at a time when men's passions and prejudices are so much inflamed, you cannot declare your sentiments even in the most modest terms without giving offence to one side or the

27

Introduction

other, which you ought carefully to avoid, as it should be your study to gain the good-will and friendship of every person your present situation connects you with; this only requires your keeping your thoughts on these subjects to yourself. There is another thing of the greatest consequence, which is, to guard against receiving prejudices which may operate so strongly as to affect your whole future conduct and put it out of your power to judge impartially upon the merits of these disputes. In time it may perhaps become your duty not to remain a silent spectator while matters of such consequence are agitating. To answer these valuable purposes, keep your thoughts or doubts, whatever they may be, to yourself, and your mind so free and disengaged from prejudice that when you are better able to judge and it may be proper for you to take a part, you may then be able, without bias, to follow the dictates of reason, truth, and duty—that God may direct you to honorable pursuits is the prayer of   Your affectionate father,

"Lewis Johnston."

Mr. Johnston's studies in Philadelphia were put a stop to by the breaking out of the Revolution, and he joined his father in Savannah, from whence they were forced to retire by the rebels having taken possession of the

Introduction

city. He and his father then came to Halifax, and the former having obtained a commission as ensign in the New York Volunteers, or Third Loyal American Regiment, was present with his regiment at the battle of Long Island, where Washington was defeated; at the subsequent taking of New York; and at the storming of Fort Montgomery, where his commander, Major Grant (the grandfather on the mother's side of Judge Haliburton, the well-known author of " Sam Slick "), was mortally wounded and died in his arms.

He was actively engaged in many other battles during the war, the last one he fought in being the battle of Eutaw Springs in 1781, where he was second in command under Major Sheridan, and where the New York Volunteers took possession of a stone house, and by well-directed fire from it repulsed the assault of the enemy, and by shooting down their gunners prevented the four six-pounders of the rebels from having any effect, thus enabling the British forces to rally and attack the Americans and convert what had almost been a defeat into a victory. Colonel Washington, a relation of General Washington, who led the Americans in the attack upon the house, was wounded and taken prisoner. Lord Edward Fitzgerald, afterward concerned in the Irish rebellion of '98, fought with his regiment in this battle, and likewise was severely wounded.

I may mention an incident connected with the defence of this stone house, exemplifying the effect of a panic upon a brave man, which was related by Captain Johnston to his daughter, my mother. Captain Johnston, in allotting posts of defence to the men of his company, placed in one of the most exposed positions one of his most reliable men, whose courage and intrepidity had been tested in many engagements, placing him at a window to keep up a fire upon the enemy. Shortly afterward, while visiting this post, he found the post deserted and the gun lying near the window. He was at a loss to account for the man's absence, but upon seeing a closet in the room he opened the door, and found the soldier hiding there. He commanded his man to come out instantly, accompanying his order with a prick from his sword. The man did so, and said: " Forgive me, Captain, this has never happened before; you have seen

me in danger behave like a man. A feeling
of panic came over me which I cannot account for. I knew if I was taken prisoner
no quarter would be shown me, as I am a
marked man; but I have known that for a
long time. Give me my gun again and I
will behave in a manner worthy of our corps."
Captain Johnston did so, and the man's subsequent conduct gave him no reason to regret it.

Captain Johnston had two brothers, Andrew and John, killed during the war. Andrew was killed while successfully leading a
company who were taking provisions to Fort
Johnston, which was besieged by the rebels.

John was taken prisoner by the enemy and
put to death in cold blood. Upon one occasion when I asked my grandmother how
my great-uncle Jack was killed, she reluct-
antly told me that he had been captured by
the rebels and put to death in an ignomini-
ous manner. I was a child at the time and
asked if they had hanged him, not regarding
her when I was told that little children should
not ask questions. She acknowledged I was
correct. I said to her: " Grandmother, when
I become a big man you must give me grand-

father's sword and I will put the rebels to death who killed him." The old lady replied that that was very wicked; that we should love our enemies and those who despitefully use us. "Besides," she added, "the debt has already been paid, for your grandfather, who was then not so good a Christian as he afterward became, took it very much to heart, for Jack was his favorite brother. For some days he was absent during the day on horseback, and returning one afternoon he said to me, 'I expect some friends here to-night, and would like supper for them at 11 o'clock; tell the negroes to have food also for their horses. I expect about twenty men.' I accordingly had supper provided, and at about eleven the company rode up to the house, dismounted, and came in. Some of them were gentlemen I knew, friends of your grandfather, but others, William, were bad-looking men, not gentlemen. After supper they remounted their horses, and your grandfather stopped a moment to put on his sword and make ready his pistols, and to bid me good-bye. I asked him when he would be back. He answered, 'Bet, if I return at all I will be back in twenty-four hours.' I slept

Introduction

little that night, and spent the next day in anxious prayer for his safe return.

"Twelve o'clock arrived, but no tidings of him. At last, about two o'clock, I heard the sound of horses riding past the house, and saw your grandfather dismount and come in. He embraced me and threw his sword and pistol on the table, both of which I could see had been used. I said to him, 'William, where have you been?' He replied, 'Bet, never ask me where I have been or what I have done, but we don't owe the rebels anything for Jack.'"

Captain Johnston and his wife must have been in New York about the time of Major André's capture, for Mrs. Johnston mentions having met him at a ball in New York about a fortnight before that event took place.

The Americans, with the assistance of France, Spain, and Holland, having obtained their independence and the rebellion having become a revolution, Captain Johnston went to Edinburgh, where he completed his medical education, which had been interrupted during the war. He then settled in Kingston, Jamaica, where he practised medicine

Introduction

until his death, which occurred December 9, 1807.

Mrs. Johnston had ten children, three of whom died in infancy. These were:

1. Andrew Lichtenstein, born in Savannah, Georgia, March 22, 1781, studied medicine in Edinburgh, and died at Kingston, Jamaica, December 2, 1805.

2. Catharine, born in Charleston, South Carolina, August 23, 1782, died in Boston, June 2, 1819.

3. Lewis, born in St. Augustine, Florida, March 10, 1784, studied medicine at Edinburgh, practised in Jamaica, and died in Wolfville, Nova Scotia.

4. John William, born in Edinburgh, May 20, 1785, died in July of the same year.

5. Elizabeth Wildman, born in Liguana, Jamaica, December 15, 1787, died at Annapolis, Nova Scotia, June 19, 1819. July 27, 1807, she was married to Thomas Ritchie, Esq., barrister, and member of the House of Assembly, afterward first Judge of the Court of Common Pleas, to whom she bore five sons and two daughters. The eldest son, John, was Solicitor-General of Nova Scotia, Senator of the Dominion of Canada, aud afterward Judge in Equity of Nova Scotia, which position he resigned shortly before his death in 1891. Her third son, Sir William Ritchie, practised law in St. John, for which county he was elected member, and was at one time Attorney-General of the Province of New Brunswick. He was afterward appointed Judge of the Supreme Court, and then became Chief Justice of the Province. This position he held until he was appointed to the Chief Justiceship of the Supreme Court of Canada, and knighted. Of the daughters, Laleah, the eldest, married Charles McColla. The second daughter, Elizabeth Lichtenstein, married in 1840

Introduction

Dr. William Johnston Almon, who was afterward member for Halifax and subsequently appointed a Senator of the Dominion. Of her three other sons, James and George studied for the Bar, and Thomas was a merchant in Cuba.

6. Laleah Peyton, born in Kingston, Jamaica, February 15, 1789, in 1814 was married to the Hon. William Bruce Almon, M.D., to whom she bore ten children. She had five sons, Hon. William J. Almon, M.D., Andrew B. Almon, barrister, James Almon, merchant, Rev. Foster H. Almon, and Lewis J. Almon, barrister. Her five daughters were : Laleah, married to Thomas Ritchie; Amelia, married to John W. Ritchie ; Eliza, married to Rev. James Ritchie ; Ella, and Mary Ann, who both died unmarried.

7. John, born in Liguana, Jamaica, January 31, 1790, studied at the High School, Edinburgh, was admitted to the Bar, and practised for some time in Jamaica. Afterward he came to Annapolis, Nova Scotia, where he was elected a member of the House of Assembly. He died at Falmouth, England, where he had gone for his health.

8. Jane Farley, born in Liguana, Jamaica, May 29, 1791, died June 4, 1793.

9. James William, born in Liguana, Jamaica, August 29, 1792, studied at the High School, Edinburgh. After he completed his studies at the High School, his mother wished to obtain a tutor for him. Lord Brougham was then a penniless young barrister in Edinburgh, and would have had the position, but Mrs. Johnston, hearing that his religious opinions were not orthodox, resolved not to engage him. After a time Mr. Johnston came out to Nova Scotia and studied law with Thomas Ritchie, of Annapolis (afterward Judge), who had married his sister Eliza. He subsequently practised in Halifax, became a partner with the Hon. S. B. Robie, and soon became the leading barrister of the Nova Scotia bar. He was ap-

Introduction

pointed a member of the Legislative Council in 1838. In 1843 he was made Attorney-General of the Province, and resigning his position in the Legislative Council, ran for Annapolis County for the Legislative Assembly. His election was obtained, and he soon became the leader of the Conservative Party in Nova Scotia, a distinction he held during the remainder of his political life, both while his party held the reins of government and when it was in opposition. His political opponent during these days was the well-known Honorable Joseph Howe. His political career terminated by his appointment, in the year 1869, to the Bench, as Judge of Equity and Judge of the Supreme Court of Nova Scotia. Owing to his declining health, in 1872 he went to the south of France, and on the death of the Hon. Mr. Howe he was appointed Governor of Nova Scotia. He soon started for home with somewhat improved health, but when he reached England he became so ill that he could proceed no further and on the 2d of November, 1873, in the eighty-first year of his age, he died at Cheltenham, where he was buried. Judge Johnston was married twice; first, to Amelia Almon, daughter of Dr. William James Almon, by whom he had six children; secondly, to Louise, widow of Captain Wentworth, R.A., by whom he had four children.

10. Jane Farley, born April 3, 1794, died in July, 1794.

RECOLLECTIONS
of a
GEORGIA LOYALIST

CHAPTER I

I WAS born May 28, 1764, in the reign of
George III., at a place called Little Ogeechee, about ten miles from Savannah, the cap-
ital of the then Province of Georgia. My
father, John Lightenstone, was born at Cronstadt in Russia. His father, Gustavus Philip
Lightenstone, was born in England, but de-
scended from a family in Germany, who write
their name " Lichtenstein." I am uncertain
whether his mother was English or Irish;
her maiden name was Beatrice Elizabeth
(if I mistake not) *Lloyd*, and my grandfather
was a Protestant minister at Cronstadt and
had an academy for young gentlemen. He
was a truly pious man, poor in this world's
goods, but rich in the inheritance of the world
to come. A letter to me from him, in answer

to one I wrote him and my grandmother when I was not eight years of age, I delight to retain as a blessed relic of the good man's prayers and blessings for his little Betsey.[1]

[1] This letter is as follows :

"SWEET TENDERLY BELOVED GRANDDAUGHTER :

" We embrace thee, we kiss thee, we give a thousand thanks, sweet creature, for thy charming, agreeable Letter, nothing can be more pleasing, nor make us so glad as thy Letter does.

" We see that thou art taking to thy Learning, and that thou art a promising dear, and we recommend to thee for a pretty companion and a true friend thy blessed Saviour; Him who cloaketh thee in apparel of the best purple, who loves thee, and all little children, and says, Suffer little children to come unto me, who when himself a little Child increased in Wisdom and Stature and in favor with God and Man. Do thou the same, and be sure to trace every step of his. May his blessings be the living waters where he thy Shepherd leads thee. We pray for this, and so do also thy Uncles and Aunts.

" Thy loving Grandfather,

G. PHILIP
and loving Grandmother,
BEATRICE ELIZABETH

LIGHTENSTONE."

Mrs. Johnston also preserved the following letter from her grandfather to her mother :

" PETERHOFF, *June*, 1769.

" MY DEAREST SWEET DAUGHTER :

" Opportunities of sending a letter are so scarce as to force one to delay what one was inclined to do the next

Recollections of a Georgia Loyalist

I have often thought that in all my back-slidings that dear saint's prayers have been heard and have been the means of my Almighty Father's mercy and forbearance with me, the vilest of sinners, who have been led by His grace and chastening to a knowledge of the truth of His Holy Word. My mother was Catherine Delegal. Her father, Philip Delegal, was of French descent, his ancestors having left France on account of being Protestants. His father was a major and died Com-

moment, and it was and is still a great grief to me to put off the answer to your charming Letter. Joy and inexpressible contentment did flow in our hearts at receiving it. This was increased as your kind and noble expressions opened to us your Christian-like sentiments, full of tenderness and affection for us. This obliges us in the highest manner, and we shall never fail to send our ardent prayers to the heavenly Throne for your everlasting happiness, and for all prosperity and health for you on this side Heaven. May God shed showers of blessings upon little Betsey, to make her grow in Wisdom and in favor with God and men; may she be bred up in the fear and love of God and her Saviour, who orders that little children shall be brought to him. Your continuing, faithful remembrance of, and tender affection towards us, will be accepted as a thing of the greatest value, and we all with the tenderest embraces do give our love to you.

"I am, dearest daughter, your truly affectionate and loving Father,

"Gustavus Philip Lightenstone."

mandant of the Island of Jersey. His son, my grandfather, went out with General Ogilthorpe, a lieutenant in his army, to Georgia upon its first settlement, took up large quantities of land there, left the army, and became one of the first settlers in that Province, where he was ultimately a man of large property. He married a Miss Daley from South Carolina. He was a man of great information, and extremely fond of reading.

When I was very young my father removed from Ogeechee to a place called Yamacraw, in the suburbs of Savannah. My father had an appointment under Government, which he held until the Revolutionary War obliged him to quit it; this was the command of a scout boat, with arms, well manned, having a large awning, and accommodation for taking the Governor or other public officers to Charleston or other adjacent places. His first duty, however, was to go to the relief of remote families who were in danger of attack from Indians, from which fact, I suppose, the boat took its name. He used also to be sent to lay quarantine at the Island of Cockspur, fifteen miles below Savannah. There was a gentleman residing on this little island with whom my father was a welcome visitor. While on duty there my father himself purchased a plantation on the Island of Skidaway, a very pleasant place upon the water, abounding in fruits of various kinds, figs, peaches, pomegranates, quinces, plums, mulberries, nectarines, and oranges; though for provisions for his family and people, he chiefly cultivated indigo and raised Indian corn and sweet potatoes. Fish, also, was easily procured in plenty, and of the finest varieties, also oysters, crabs, prawn, and shrimps.

We had a house in Savannah, where I was early put to school, and from being an only child my intellect was probably developed more quickly, I being thrown very much upon my own resources. When in the country I found in the trees, the river, the animals, much to amuse and occupy my leisure hours, and my parents conversed with me and stimulated my taste for reading, by making me read good authors to them. Having a good memory and uncommon love for reading, I found pleasure in books that would perhaps in this present age be too dry for a child of seven or eight years of age. For instance, I once read a book the title of which in after life I had no recollection of, except from its mentioning that part of the twentieth chapter of St. John where that most touching and interesting passage was of Mary Magdalene's going to the tomb to discover her Lord. Not seeing the body she turned with a heavy and disappointed heart to make inquiry of her blessed Lord Himself, whom she took to be the gardener. His "Mary!" her answer, and no doubt Mary's look, soon made Him known to His faithful, sorrowing disciple. Such was the effect of this book on my infant mind that forty years after, when I had the book with some others sent me to read, as soon as I looked into it I remembered the passage that had struck me and exclaimed to my children, "This is the book!" The title was "Gilbert West on the Resurrection," and I have now the copy, which the lady politely requested my acceptance of, she having another copy besides.

My mother, not being in good health, was once recommended to pass a summer in Philadelphia, and to relieve her of all care I was to remain with my father. The vessel in which the passengers were to embark lay fifteen miles below Savannah, and the evening

Recollections of a Georgia Loyalist

before she sailed I went down with some ladies
who were going, expecting to return with my
father next day when he took my mother down.
When they arrived I showed so much grief at
parting from her, that my poor mother was
much distressed, and my father would have returned for my clothes. The wind, however,
being fair, put this out of the question, and he
consented to my going with only one suit, the
ladies offering to assist in cutting over some
of my mother's clothes for me. In this way
little Betsey, then about seven years of age,
made her *début* on the wide ocean, which it
has since so often been her lot to traverse.

On our return from Philadelphia we resided
between town and country, and when at the
former I attended school. My mother died
when I was turned ten years of age, and I
felt her loss keenly. Shortly after, my father
at the request of an aunt of my mother's,
Mrs. Richard, sent me to reside with her in
Savannah, where I attended the best schools
in the place. My aunt did me every justice
in bringing me up, and endeavored to make
me a notable needlewoman, in which art she
herself excelled, but my love for reading was
so much greater than for sewing that I often

had a book under my work to look into as opportunity offered. The good old lady not being able to make me perfect in sewing, declared at last that I should never be anything but a botcher at it, yet I did not think I really deserved the charge.

In 1774 the Revolutionary War commenced at Boston and began to spread to the southward. In '76 the people in Georgia were inflamed against the Government of Great Britain, and were raising a ragged corps of all sorts. Some had guns with firelocks and some without, and all, gentle and simple, were made to declare whether they were on the side of the King or for the people whom we Loyalists, then termed Tories, called rebels. If a Tory refused to join the people, he was imprisoned, and tarred and feathered. This was a terrible indignity, the poor creature being stripped naked, tarred all over, and then rolled in feathers. I might once, if I would have gone to the window, have seen a poor man carried all over the town with the mob around him, in such a plight, but the idea was too dreadful. He was an inoffensive man, a British pilot.

Our teachers became officers in the rebel

army, and everywhere the scum rose to the top. All the public officers under Government remained loyal and quit the country, their estates being confiscated and afterward sold. My father, at the barking of a dog while he was shaving and preparing to dress that he might escape in his boat, looked up and saw an armed party near the house. He had just time to go through a door that opened into the garden, leap the fence, and lay himself down at a little distance in some tall grass which concealed him. He could hear the soldiers talking loudly to his servants and saying that he could not be far off, for his clothes and watch were in the room. If he was above ground, they said, they would surely have him. My father had a sensible, plausible black man, who had been brought up as a pet in my grandfather's house, and who was greatly attached to the family. He contrived to amuse the soldiers in different ways, while he got down his sails and oars to take them to a back landing-place, where the boat lay. The leader of the party was a fine young man, a Mr. John Milledge, whom my father had known from his infancy, and who some years afterward was at Augusta with the rank of colonel. He was an amiable man, and his turning against my father served to show the spirit of the times and the violence with which civil wars are entered upon.

After their unsuccessful pursuit, the party returned, and my father got to his boat without delay and arrived at Tybee, where the British man-of-war, the *Scarborough*, lay. Then he embarked, as did my future husband, who had also been fortunate enough to effect his escape to Tybee, and they sailed for Halifax, Nova Scotia, in 1776. At that time I was twelve years of age, and being with my aunt on the mainland, at her plantation, did not take leave of my father or know what was going on at Skidaway until some time after I heard he was gone. Commissioners were appointed to confiscate the Loyalists' property and dispose of it as being forfeited because of their not joining the rebels, and my grandfather had a petition drawn up which he made me take, accompanied by a lady (sorely against my will, for I felt so indignant at their treatment of my father), to the Board of Commissioners, which set forth the orphan condition I was left in, and petitioned that my

Recollections of a Georgia Loyalist

father's property might be given to me. This request I have every reason to think was acceded to, as our property was not sold as was that of many other Loyalists. One or two cases besides mine show that they did give the property to wives and children whose husbands and fathers had been forced away as mine had been.

My father and Mr. Johnston left Halifax for New York, the former there entering the Quartermaster-General's department, the latter joining a Provincial Corps (the New York Volunteers) composed of Loyalists, which was actively engaged during the war, never being kept in garrison duty. This regiment was twice new officered, its first officers, with a few exceptions, falling on the field of battle. Major Grant, who had taken Mr. Johnston under his care and was like a father to him, was killed in storming Fort Montgomery, and my husband felt his loss severely. At the close of 1778, Colonel Campbell, who was afterward knighted and made governor of Madras, in India, was sent with three thousand men to take Georgia. The New York Volunteers was one of the regiments, and Col. C., knowing that my father had resided a great part of his life in that Province, took him into his service as an adviser and guide where best to effect a landing. The town was taken without loss, though the Americans as they retreated wantonly fired on the 71st Regiment of Highlanders, without attempting a regular stand. This exposed the inhabitants to the fury of the British soldiers, who then felt as though they were taking the place by storm. In consequence, before the officers could have time to stop them they committed much outrage, ripped open feather beds, destroyed the public papers and records, and scattered everything about the streets. Numbers of the enemy were taken in a swamp a few miles from Savannah. While Mr. Johnston was with his company in the pursuit he saw his father at his own door, and had only time to go up to Colonel Maitland and request that he would put a guard at his father's house to secure his safety from the enraged troops, who knew not friend from foe. Colonel Maitland had been the early friend and college companion of my father-in-law, Dr. Johnston, in Edinburgh, and meeting with his son at New York was like a father to him and did all he could to serve him.   He, of course, placed a guard there.

My father in a few days sent a passport for myself and my aunt to come to town.   I was then in my fifteenth year, and new to scenes of the kind, and having to stop within a mile of Savannah that the Hessian officer on duty there should examine our pass, I was dreadfully frightened.   He soon allowed us to go on; and what a sight did the streets present of feathers and papers!

The meeting with my father I scarce need add was joyful.   I was there made acquainted with my father's bosom friend, Mr. McCulloch.   He was a widower, a very handsome man for his time of life, and had two daughters in England, one of whom is now Mrs. Roupell.   He was very fond of me, and I suppose looked on me as a child, but I felt an affection for him for a short time that I can hardly define.   He was very amiable; if I wanted any money he would, if my father gave me a guinea, always say, "Give her another," or if my foolish young head fancied, as it did at times, some article of dress, he was always ready to second my wish. Yet my father idolized me too much to need

49

that any should ask for me. I loved him, yet I always from a child had an awe of him. My dear, indulgent mother was perhaps too yielding to her only child, and but for his strictness to me, for which I am now grateful, she might have spoilt me. She was too good a woman to have overlooked faults of the heart and mind, yet this I am sensible of, that I could take advantage of her, when a word from my father was enough. On one occasion when the cat ate my bird I was so angry that I went to beat her. My mother tried to prevent me, and finding me obstinate and persistent, was going to correct me as I deserved, but I ran away and got up into a big tree out of reach, and perhaps she had no great wish to use violence in getting me down. In a short time I saw my father coming along the road, when I was soon out of the tree and seated in the parlor.

We may see in almost every event that befalls us the hand of our merciful Heavenly Father directing the various events of our lives for our good. Perhaps had my beloved and tender mother lived she might not have kept as strict a hand over me as my volatile nature required. My aunt was kind, but was at the same time decided in her conduct toward me, and I was made industrious at my needle. Other parts of education I required no stimulus in, as I liked them better; indeed I was always ambitious to be at the head of my class at school.

CHAPTER II

AFTER Savannah was taken I remained with my aunt the greater part of the time, but at last my father was requested by Mrs. Johnston to bring me to town to pass a few weeks with her daughter. This he did, and I appeared, a young unsophisticated girl, quite new to the world, its customs and usages. On my arrival Mrs. Johnston's son came hastily into the room, which he had left a little before to seek for his watch. When he entered he merely glanced round the room and retreated. I, a little rustic, in my simple dress, which my fond aunt and I had made at her place called "Mount Piety" (a name she took from the "Pilgrim's Progress" when she purchased her plantation), must have looked strange to the gay Captain Johnston, who had lately been among the dashing fashionables of New York, then remarkable (during Sir H. Clinton's rule) for its elegance and dissipation. No wonder, I sometimes think, that I should at once have caught his eye. At the steps he met my father coming in, and asked him what girl that was in the parlor. My father said, "Your sister, and Miss Stewart, our former teacher." "No," was the reply, "there was another." My father said, "No one but my Betsey," and my husband has often spoken since of the meeting, and said that the thought at once came to him that I would be *his* Betsey, although an hour before had any one talked to him of marrying he would have assured him it was a thing out of the question. He had resisted all the beauty and fashion he had left, and found something in a simple child of nature to make him not many weeks after change his sentiments. Such was the romance of the olden times!

I remained with Mrs. Johnston some weeks, and it was some time before I could get over my bashful timidity. Every day there were several officers dining at Dr. Johnston's; having two sons in the army and being loyal he thought they could not show too much attention to those who had rescued us from rebel power. I was glad to get into the drawing-room before they arrived; and to take wine at dinner with one of these gay soldiers called a deep blush into my cheeks, it was all so unlike the ways at Mount Piety. My father perceived rather more attention to me than he wished from Captain Johnston, for being intimately acquainted with him and knowing his sentiments on that head, he did not suspect him of any thoughts of marriage. Accordingly, unwilling that I should be trifled with, he told me one evening, on my returning from a drive to see a lady, that I must be prepared to go back in the morning to my aunt's. This was rather a damper to my youthful heart, and no less so to the companion of my drive, and he contrived to find opportunity that evening to say what has been said so often to other silly girls, I suppose. By silence only I told him what I felt, then I got upstairs into my own room in the dark, and wept most abundantly, not at the thought of parting from him, but to think I should have listened to such a thing without my father's knowledge. I was obliged to dry my tears and go down to supper, but I went with a heavy heart. Next morning I left Savannah and did not enjoy my home as formerly.

A few days after, a circumstance occurred

WILLIAM MARTIN JOHNSTON, M.D.

that might have had serious consequences to the honour of my husband, had not my aunt's stiff notions of female decorum prevented. He had ridden out a few miles to visit a lady with whom we were acquainted, and had prevailed on her to drive to my aunt's plantation and request her to allow me to accompany her back to remain a day or two. My aunt was inexorable and declined my going, and after their departure she very properly pointed out her reasons for refusing, saying that it would look as if I wished to go because of Captain Johnston's being there. In her opinion such a thing would not be delicate. Whether she convinced me then I will not say, but this I now know, she was right and had proper ideas of female reserve. Captain Johnston being disappointed of my company rose early the next morning and left his kind friends sooner than he would have done had I been there, and returned to Savannah. But what was his mortification and dismay when he got there, to find that by a sudden order his regiment with some other troops had embarked at daylight for Carolina on an expedition. He never stopped at his father's, but rode down to a wharf to try to get a boat to follow and if possible join them before their landing. A ship's boat was there with two seamen who were to return without delay to their captain, but the earnestness with which he and our friend Mr. McCulloch urged them, and the Captain's offer of the only two guineas he had about him, and his watch, softened Jack's heart. One said to the other, "We won't take the gentleman's watch, only the money," and went at all risks with him. He felt his honour at stake from being absent at the time, and especially as he knew his major was not on good terms with him and would gladly avail himself of such an opportunity to put him under arrest, a disgrace which his proud spirit could not have borne. Fortunately, he caught up with his regiment before they landed and went to Colonel Maitland and told his case, fearing greatly that the major would put him under arrest. Colonel Maitland did away with his apprehensions by giving him the forlorn hope, a post of danger and honour, and he was the first man to land. Had I gone to Mrs. Houston's he would have remained longer, and what misery it would have given him! He was away three months in the interior of South Carolina, and the troops returned to us, as was too much the case in that ill-fated war, without doing anything. Colonel Prevost, I think, commanded; a different man from his brother, the General.

In September, 1779, the French fleet, under the command of Count D'Estaing arrived at Tybee, and shortly after landed some miles from Savannah at a place called Buhlah. There they spent some time in gradual approaches and in throwing up battlements before the town, forming a regular siege, which gave Colonel Moncrief, our brave engineer, time also to throw up works. Though the lines were very extensive, and the British force very small, not above 1,800 men (Colonel Maitland was in Carolina with 500 men), such was Moncrief's ardor, skill, and industry that he made the town able to stand a siege of six weeks. The French and Americans were 10,000 strong, and they were opening their batteries, and constantly cannonading and throwing bomb shells. Fortunately, however, our men were encamped near the trenches, and these deadly shells went a distance over their heads. The streets being sandy and not paved, the shells fell and made great holes in the sand, which often put out the fuse and prevented explosion. Indeed, the colored children got so used to the shells that they would run and cover them with sand, and as we were rather scarce of ammunition they would often pick up the spent balls and get for them seven-pence apiece.

Soon almost every family was removed from the town to an island opposite, where they made use of barns, and taking their bedding and some furniture divided it by portions. In the barn where I was there were fifty-eight women and children, all intimate friends, and who had each one or more near relatives in the lines. My mother-in-law had two sons, I had my father and one very dear to me, my future husband. Only one male friend was with us, Dr. Johnston, too old to fight, though his whole heart was in the cause. Every other house and barn besides the one we occupied was full of females. The General sent a flag to Count D'Estaing to request that he would allow Mrs. Prevost and her children to go on board one of our ships to be in a safe place. The request was refused, and she remained in a cellar in Savannah, which was made bomb proof with feather beds. Fortunately, though their hope was by the incessant fire to burn the town and force a surrender, a merciful God protected us and defeated their intention. Only one house took fire, and that was opposite the one Mrs. Prevost and her children were in; I cannot now remember whether the flames were subdued or the house consumed. Wet blankets and other means were taken to guard the opposite house from taking fire; the streets were broad.

Our men, having few to relieve them, suffered from fatigue and want of rest, but in the height of our despondence Colonel Maitland effected a junction in a wonderful manner, crossed from the Carolina side, and with his 500 soldiers entered Savannah, thus giving new life and joy to the worn-out troops. Previous to the commencement of the siege, Dr. Johnston with all the females of his family went to the island. Mrs. Johnston, however, remained longer. She had two sons then in the lines, one a captain in the New York Volunteers the other a captain in Brown's Rangers, who were stationed at different parts of the lines. She had also two younger sons, one in his fifteenth the other in his tenth year, whom their brothers had wished to be allowed to take with them. This Mrs. Johnston would not hear of. She had two sons in posts of danger, and she could not bear to risk more. I chose to remain with her, for an obvious reason, I had thus an opportunity of often seeing her son William when he visited her.

One day he came in haste to say we must move from the town as quickly as possible, for the enemy were about to open their batteries on it. This we did immediately, but before we had got far they commenced a heavy cannonade, which was kept up for two hours. The shot was whistling about our ears and I was sadly frightened, ducking my head as if that could save me. My heroic mother-in-law stopped suddenly and addressed her boys: "My sons, I was about to disgrace you; go join your brothers." Alex went to William, and John to Andrew, the older brothers being scarcely able to believe that their mother had sent them. Soon we got safely to the wharf, and then over to the island, the name of which was Hutchinson Island. It was all cultivated and settled; rice was the grain raised, and as the crop had to be for a certain time, during the process of culture, kept under water, the town was most unhealthy, every one in autumn suffering from that dreadful disease fever and ague. Of late years, I am told, they have drained the island, given up the culture of rice, and planted cotton, corn, etc., instead, a change which has greatly improved the health of the people.

After a siege of some weeks the concentrated forces of French and Americans, 10,-000 men against our handful, fearful of a British fleet coming and blocking up or taking their ships, and dreading the risk of storms at that season, made, on the 9th of October, 1779, a grand attack with small arms on our works at the dawn of day. Alas, every heart in our barn was aching, every eye in tears! When they sent their flag to offer terms, though our General was told that no quarter would be given if he refused, that they would take the garrison by storm, and that he would have the lives of his men to answer for, he refused to capitulate. Captain William Johnston met the officer, the Count de Noailles, and conducted him to headquarters, and was present when he gave the above message in an elegant style, contrasting strongly with our plain, blunt Swiss or German. The answer the Count received was laconic, " The King, my Master, pays these men to fight, and they must fight, and we decline your terms." Therefore, we had reason to be afflicted, not daring to anticipate a victory with such fearful odds. The Almighty and Gracious God did, however, assist us, and we conquered, though no men could have behaved more gallantly than the French. One poor fellow planted his colors three times on one of our redoubts, but the third time he fell.

Our anxiety to hear about our friends may well be imagined, but we soon had great reason for gratitude and praise. None of our relatives and friends were killed or wounded, though all were much fatigued from many weeks' want of rest, and from that day's action. We had stock of all descriptions, and many a harmless animal and turkey was killed and prepared, to send over to our friends. The Polish rebel, Count Pulaski, who joined the Americans, was killed that morning. One battery was manned with seamen, who behaved most gallantly. Had the enemy not apprehended danger to their fleet by remaining, in all probability they would have renewed their attack, and it was not thought possible we could have had strength to defeat them again.

When we got into the town it offered a desolate view. The streets were cut into deep holes by the shells, and the houses were riddled with the rain of cannon balls. Winter was now approaching and many houses were not habitable, so Dr. Johnston with his family took a house out of town until his was repaired.

CHAPTER III

I WAS married in Savannah, November 21, 1779, then fifteen and a half years old; my husband, William Martin Johnston, being twenty-five and a half. Some months after, he was attacked with a nervous complaint, brought on by great fatigue in the special service of taking information orally to some of our troops in garrison at Augusta, a hundred and thirty miles from Savannah. He rode night and day through an enemy's country, accomplished his mission, and returned immediately, never but once alighting from his horse. Though then young, strong, and active, his constitution long suffered from the effects of the journey. He went for a few weeks to St. Augustine, East Florida, to try the change, but not getting well, he was recommended to New York, and it was thought advisable that I should remain in Savannah.

When the day came for him to go, the ship lay at Tybee, where he and his sister, Mrs.

Recollections of a Georgia Loyalist

Farley, with her husband and child, were to embark. Mr. Farley was then in a deep decline. The next morning I was sitting very disconsolate in my own room, in tears, no doubt thinking that our separation was for me the climax of misery, for we were both strongly tinctured with the romance of the old school, when who should enter but my husband. The wind not being favorable, he had risked its changing and his losing his passage, to come up for me. One half-hour was all I had in which to pack up, and notwithstanding I had to get my husband's linen ready (part of my own was lying wet) and arrange other matters, we were off before Mr. Johnston's good father returned from sitting in the Council, of which he was then President. My father-in-law was as angry, I fancy, as his mild nature would admit, at his son's romantic folly.

It was the month of June, 1780, and we had a fine ship. At Charleston we put ourselves under the convoy of Sir Henry Clinton's fleet and army, Sir Henry being about to return, after the reduction of Charleston, to New York. The voyage from thence to New York took us only eight days. We had

pleasant weather, bands of music were playing on board the different ships, and the
whole trip was very delightful.

At New York we landed, and we spent the
hot months on Long Island. In October we
left with a fleet and force under command of
General Leslie, who was going up the Chesapeake. We took our passage in a private
vessel, as the captain assured us there were
a number of private armed vessels going on
to Charleston that would protect us, and that
he would not go in with the fleet. All this,
we found afterward, was untrue; the captain
took us up the Chesapeake, and we lay five
weeks near Portsmouth, opposite Norfolk,
which then had only the walls of the houses
standing, having been burnt by the Governor, Lord Dunmore, on his being obliged to
quit. Mr. and Mrs. Farley remained on
board the same vessel to go on, but we were
to remain through the winter, I having the
prospect of becoming a mother in March.
In the same extraordinary manner as our
public affairs were ever conducted, however,
just as the poor people came forward to show
their loyalty, in the hope that the British
troops would remain permanently there, sud-

denly in the month of November the General's aid-de-camp, Major Skelly, came to tell Mr. Johnston that the troops would embark next morning. This took us unprepared in every way. The major said he would get us a good passage in a transport, and as there was little time to get provisions, he kindly said he would send us a good supply of dead and some live poultry and stock. Our poor landlady, a Mrs. Elliot, sat with her head back and her mouth extended, scarce in her senses from the shock, till at last she found speech to articulate: "Well, this is the third time we have been so served by the British. We have shown our loyalty, and they have left us to the rage and persecution of the Americans for doing them service."

Our passage was rough and tedious. The vessel Mrs. Farley was in separated from the fleet, and within a day's sail of Charleston was captured by a privateer, who took all the provisions, and indeed everything its crew could see, even to the compass. I suppose they thought the vessel too insignificant to man, so they allowed her in that state to proceed. Fortunately, she arrived the next day, and Mr. Farley died a day or

two after the party landed. We arrived a
week later, and he was then buried. Had
they remained with the fleet the poor wife
would have been doubly distressed from her
husband's dying at sea. Fortunately, she
had also the consolation of finding her second
brother Lewis there, who attended to everything. Here my husband and I had to part,
as he was obliged to join his regiment, and I
returned to Savannah. My brother Lewis,
with Mrs. Farley and family and myself, went
in a large boat with an awning, under which
there was good accommodation for sleeping.
The voyage to Savannah was inland, and every
night we stopped in some river or creek, pro-
ceeding at daylight. We were sadly annoyed
by mosquitoes in these places. At last we got
in safety to Savannah, where my sister had an
affecting meeting with her father and family.
There she was told of the death of her brother,
Captain Andrew Johnston. He had fallen at
Augusta after gallantly succeeding in a sortie
the troops were forced to make to procure
provisions they much needed, and which he
had bravely offered to undertake. In returning he had received a shot in his back, which
was fatal. His good father was sitting with

Recollections of a Georgia Loyalist

the Governor in Council, when a countryman came down, told of a skirmish our people had had with the rebels, and was asked if any were killed. The reply, "None but Captain Johnston," was a shock too great for the father's tender feelings, and he of course immediately returned home.

I remained for some time in much anxiety for my husband's safety, as his regiment was in active service. Before my confinement he obtained leave, his regiment being then in quarters, to come for a short time to Savannah. My son, who was named Andrew after his brave uncle, was born March 22, 1781. His father returned to Charleston soon after, and a few months later, from the enemy's troops coming near the town and rendering it unsafe to go many miles from it, the Governor, Sir James Wright, with the advice of his Council, thought it expedient to raise some three troops of horse at the expense of the Province. Upon his father's application my husband was appointed to one of these and to command the whole. Of the three, my father had one and Captain Campbell Wylly another. Mr. Johnston would not accept the command unless he got leave to keep his rank and situation and pay in his regiment, which he obtained. As captain of a troop of horse he had fifteen shillings per day with passage money, and how happy did I think I should be when I had him so near me. But like all human enjoyments, mine was not full and satisfactory. My husband was now more exposed to danger than before; upon any alarm the dragoons were sent out and the gates locked, and every third night he in turn was out on horseback with his party, the gates being locked and *chevaux de frise* put up to them, and remained on the lookout until three or four in the morning. I have often of a very cold winter's night known his hair quite stiff with icicles. The troops were afterward sent to Great Ogeechee, about thirty or forty miles from Savannah.

Reports daily came in that the enemy meant to surprise them, and the Commander-in-Chief, General Clarke (afterward Sir Alured Clarke), sent messages every day to that effect so that the men were worn out for want of rest. At last they began to think they had no intention of attacking them, and one day when they were off their guard and most of the men were in the yard, there suddenly appeared at the edge of the wood about 300 of the enemy drawn up. Our men then got in as fast as possible and made what preparation time would allow. As many as had arms were placed on a boarded piazza, ready when the order was given to fire. Their captain making them reserve their first fire, the enemy fired, happily, however, without effect. Then Captain Johnston ordered his men to fire, which they did, and with such effect as to bring down three officers and some men, I believe. After a while the enemy drew off, and an express was sent on a fleet horse to let Colonel Campbell know the captain's perilous state and request his coming to his assistance. The man, deceiving the rebels by making a feint as if he were a deserter, went slowly, but as soon as he came near them clapped spurs to his horse and soon got out of their reach. Colonel Campbell did not come as quickly as he ought, or he might have saved the lives of many of our gallant little troop. He did come many hours after, however, and got the troop under arms and went out to meet the foe. He left our men in the most dangerous position, and being bad horsemen they suffered greatly. My husband, however, escaped unhurt, and the enemy retired.

When the news came to Savannah, though I knew he was safe, the thought of the danger he had been in overpowered my mind, and I sought relief on my knees by offering prayers and thanksgivings with lively gratitude to my Heavenly Father for His great mercy in sparing the husband and the father. Not many months after, Georgia was given up, and in July, 1782, Savannah was evacuated and the troops went to Charleston. Some of Mr. Johnston's early friends whom he knew at Philadelphia, one a Major Fishbaune in the American army, who had an interview with him during a cessation of arms, requested him to leave me, and said I should have every kindness and protection and be secure in our house until I was fitter for moving. I knew my husband would not like the separation, and I positively refused to remain, but I have no doubt that had I stayed my father's property would have been given up to me through the interest of those friends.

CHAPTER IV

WE went to Charleston early in July, and the 23d of August, 1782, my second child, a daughter called Catherine after my mother, was born. I first became acquainted there with the Roupell family. The present Mr. G. Roupell's father was then Postmaster-General, and lived very handsomely. I resided with my father's old friend Mr. McCulloch and his good wife (who was a Miss Roupell) about three weeks. We were very handsomely billeted in a fine house belonging to one of the rebel gentlemen who had left town. In December the war was drawing to a close, Charleston was evacuated, and my husband was obliged to go with his regiment to New York. His father and family had gone from Georgia to St. Augustine, and Mr. Johnston thought it better for me to go there to his father until his regiment was disbanded and he could come to me. With my two little ones I embarked with a nurse on board a small schooner for St. Augustine.

Recollections of a Georgia Loyalist

We arrived there safely with many more Loyalists, though we saw many vessels lying stranded along the shore that had been wrecked on the sand bar. Fortunately, however, no lives were lost, though much of the poor Loyalists' property was destroyed. We got over with only once thumping on the bar.

The town of St. Augustine lies low; it is pleasantly situated upon the sea, the air is very salubrious, and it has long been the resort of invalids in search of health. The citadel is a fine, strong one, and affords a delightful promenade upon the ramparts, which are wide and elevated. The chief inhabitants at the time I was there were Greeks from Smyrna and Minorca, brought there by a Dr. Turnbull to cultivate his lands at the Metanges, some miles from St. Augustine. He married a lady of Smyrna, who always retained the costume of her country, a majestic, noble-looking woman. These people, not agreeing with Dr. Turnbull, settled about the town and were the only persons who cultivated gardens or reared poultry. Fish, which was in great abundance, was our chief dependence and our ration, but I never was in better

Lewis Johnston, Jr., M.D.

health and indeed never was so fleshy as during my sixteen months' residence there. My husband paid us a visit in 1783, but as the war was then closing and the peace of 1783 was about taking place, he could not be long from his regiment. His father, judging that with a growing family his half-pay would not go far, advised him to go to Edinburgh and prosecute his medical studies, which he had early commenced at Philadelphia under his father's friend Dr. Rush, and which had been interrupted by the breaking out of the rebellion.

In the spring of 1784 we had notice that Florida was ceded to the Spaniards and that St. Augustine would soon be evacuated. My third child Lewis was born, March 10, 1784, and the end of May, my father-in-law, having a transport appointed for his sole use, to go wherever he wished in the British Dominions, chose his native land, and we embarked on the 25th of May for Greenock. My husband had gone before in the *Diomede* frigate, with some invalids under his command, for Portsmouth, England, intending soon after to proceed to Edinburgh. We had not a long but we had a dangerous passage; the vessel was worm-eaten from lying long in the river, the tar and turpentine, that Dr. Johnston's slaves had made on a plantation he had, leaked out in the storms we encountered and choked the pumps, and at one time we had four feet of water in the hold. From having little other ballast than the tar and turpentine we were in danger of upsetting, and accordingly we put into the Cove of Cork for ballast and to repair the cable, and remained a week in that beautiful harbor.

When we arrived at Greenock we found the principal inn very full, and I with Rachel, a younger sister of Mr. Johnston, and my nurse and three children, were put into the attic story. As we had never before been in a place of such bustle and stir, we were rather alarmed and could not sleep. To add to our fears suddenly about midnight a female servant with a candle abruptly opened the door and asked if Captain Johnston's lady was there. "Why, what do you want? I am Mrs. Johnston," I answered, hardly knowing what I said. With perfect composure she replied, "Then you can make room for the Captain." And, sure enough, it was my husband, who had unexpectedly arrived. He knew we were to sail for Scotland, and he was going to Edinburgh to await our arrival. Dr. Johnston had written to a gentleman in Edinburgh, mentioning our arrival, and Mr Johnston, who had letters of introduction to the same person, happened to be with him when the doctor's letter was received. My husband then immediately took a post-chaise and drove rapidly to Greenock, a distance of seventy miles, but not setting out early from Edinburgh, did not reach Greenock until twelve at night. Stopping at the inn where we were, he was told he could not be accommodated for it was very full and they had not a single bed. He was turning away to find another inn, when the woman happened to say there was a very large family from America there. It struck him, as he often humorously said in relating the adventure, that he might get *half* a bed. The woman found out where I was, and he was close behind her when she spoke to me. We were all crowded into a miserable little room, and the children were not very quiet after their voyage, so that only the pleasure of meeting his family could counterbalance Mr. Johnston's want of comfort. Next day he took me and our little family on, his father with his family remaining a few days at Greenock to recruit.

We stopped at Glasgow part of a day, and next morning set out for Edinburgh, where we settled at Rosebank, a sweet place my husband had taken for his father, about a mile from the city to the south. It was well entitled to the name it bore, as roses clambered all over the front of the house and completely covered it. They were then in bloom, and there were also two pretty flower gardens, one on each side of the house. The place answered very delightfully during the summer and autumn, but when the roads got heavy and miry, and winter was commencing, we found it would not do to walk so great a distance. The Episcopal Chapel was in the old town, and Dr. Johnston, a poor Loyalist who had lost so much by the war, could not afford a carriage. He therefore let Rosebank, and took until May a house in George's Square. When that time expired we removed to the new town, in James Street, the road that looks down upon Leith Walk, then quite a fashionable place.

As I expected to be confined in May, when

the family would be removing, I took a lodg-
ing in Bristol Street for a month, and May
20, 1785, gave birth to a fine boy, whom we
called John William. Mrs. Farley stayed with
me until I could remove. My husband attended college all the winter, and in the spring
went to London to attend the hospitals there
and to form some plan as to where he should
finally practice. He had handsome offers
made him by Sir Archibald Campbell, who
was the Colonel Campbell who commanded
in Georgia, and for whom, when he was
an officer under him, he volunteered that
journey on horseback which I have already
mentioned, which for a time so greatly injured
his health. Colonel Campbell was going to
India as Governor of Madras, and would have
taken my husband and probably put him in
the way of making his fortune. About
that time, however, Sir Alured Clarke was
made Governor of Jamaica, and thither that
and other circumstances led him to fix on
going.

When my babe was three months old it
pleased our Heavenly Father to take him from
a world of sin and sorrow. He had the
thrush, or spine, as the Scots term it, most

virulently. Dr. Wardrope was our surgeon,
Dr. Johnston attended, and they called in
Dr. Gregory, but all without avail. Mr.
Johnston went that autumn to Kingston, and
I left Edinburgh in October, 1786. I had
met with much kindness and affection in that
city, and one friend especially I felt grieved
to part from. In our youthful days, I only
twenty and Mrs. Davidson a little more, we
met as strangers at a dinner party, and took
a great fancy to each other's faces. She
called on us next day, and from that time to
her death we were as attached as the fondest
of sisters ever were. During my two years
in Edinburgh we were much together.

I left my own father, who accompanied me
to Greenock, as did Mrs. Farley, dear, good
woman, and took my Kitty and Lewis, both
then very young, Dr. Johnston keeping Andrew to be with him and to be educated in
Edinburgh. I arrived in Kingston, December 15, 1786, and found my husband well,
though he had been ill with the common
fevers of the place. December 15, 1787, my
beloved Eliza was born, and February 15,
1789, my dear Laleah Peyton was added to
my family. The 31st of January, 1790, my

son John was born. Jane Farley, a sweet blossom, was born in 1791, and died June 4, 1793, of malignant sore throat and scarlet fever. My son James William was born August 29, 1792.

CHAPTER V

SOON after, the yellow fever was brought to Jamaica from Philadelphia and made great havoc among all new-comers and sailors. Strange to tell, however, it never attacked those who had resided there for any length of time, nor of course the natives, but all strangers and the poor seamen were carried off in great numbers. Sometimes there were seventeen or more funerals a day. My husband, having an extensive practice, had a great deal to do with the sickness, for in Kingston whatever merchants the doctors attend they have the attendance of all on the ships consigned to them. The disease quite baffled human skill; still some medical men were more successful than others. Soon a war of words and angry disputations broke out in the newspapers between two of our proud physicians, Drs. Grant and Hanis. The former held bleeding as the best treatment, the latter calomel, and Hanis got a list of all the cases of the different practitioners

HON. JUDGE JAMES WILLIAM JOHNSTON
In 1873 Governor-elect of Nova Scotia

with an account of the treatment they had received. Few doctors were for the lancet; my husband's treatment was to a great extent calomel, and his recoveries were more than could have been looked for. Happily, neither Dr. Johnston nor myself nor any of my family took the disease.

I should have mentioned that on my husband's arrival, previous to my going out, he was most kindly received by Sir Alured Clarke, and was told that if he thought of settling in Spanish Town he should be happy to have him an inmate at the King's House until his family came out. The Governor attached him nominally to some regiment, merely to give him a commission to receive island pay, 20s. per week for himself, 10s. for me, and 5s. for each of the children, which he retained as long as he chose. If one regiment left he got appointed to another, and I never knew him called on but once (when the surgeon was absent) to attend a punishment in Kingston Barracks. The Governor also introduced him to two gentlemen in particular, who were ever his warm friends. One was Dr. Weir, Physician-General to the forces, a man of high character, and the other, Mr. James Wildman, a man of large fortune and one of the Council, who, besides his income as attorney to all the estates of Mr. Beckford of Fonthill, England, made £10,000 a year. Mr. Wildman made Mr. Johnston an offer of the attendance of his estates near Kingston, in St. Andrew's parish, Liguana. As there were several established medical men in Spanish Town, my husband accepted Mr. Wildman's offer and settled in Liguana near Halfwaytree.

When I arrived I was shown great kindness by Mr. and Mrs. Wildman, and at their request they became sponsors to my beloved Eliza Wildman, as they wished the child to bear their name. In 1794, April 3d, my last child was born. Her father's partiality to his sister Mrs. Farley led him to call her Jane Farley. When three months old she was inoculated for the smallpox, as her father being so much where it was, though she was young thought this the only chance to prevent her taking it. What she had proved the confluent, and after lying on my lap for some time on a pillow, a very sad spectacle, one sore being quite black, she died in my arms. She, as well as the other

84

Recollections of a Georgia Loyalist

Jane, was a beautiful child, with angelic blue eyes and a countenance which showed that she was not meant to sojourn upon this earth. After her death I was much exhausted in mind and body, having no female relation to be with me, only black servants, and having to think about and direct everything for so many little ones. As soon as her father took the dear angel out of my lap I got into another room, and there on my knees poured out my supplications for aid and support, that I might bear the stroke with a resigned will. Yet I had not the same light of truth that I have received since my bodily blindness, though still I am fain to hope divine grace led me then to the footstool of mercy, where I have been accustomed to seek aid through all my life. Yet, oh, what a backslider I have been! How often and how much have I failed in my duty!

When I went to Jamaica I felt greatly the want of religious example, and I found that even the preaching was cold morality. Morals there were at the lowest ebb, cards were played on Sunday, and dinner parties were given on that sacred day. It is very different now, and much of the improved state of re-

ligion and morality is owing to the Scotch
churches and the preaching of the Dissenters,
which has been the means of awaking many
a poor soul, and has led the blacks to more
moral habits of life. Perhaps, with the blessing of God these dreadful examples led me to
greater strictness than I might have used in
a country less decided. I used to be diligent
in teaching my children and reading to them
every morning from the old "Whole Duty of
Man" and conducting family prayers while
they knelt around me. I taught all to read
and the girls to sew. They were not at a
school until I went for my health, after ten
years' residence there, again to Edinburgh.
My time was greatly devoted to my family,
and though but twenty-two when I went to
Jamaica I was at only one Assembly and two
private dances during my life there. Very
soon I got my husband to promise not to
have company on Sunday, which he did readily, as he highly respected my religious principles and had the utmost confidence in my
mode of bringing up my children, nor did he
ever interfere with my discipline. I taught
the children to love the truth, and to obey,
and I can with pleasure say that their hearts

were mine, and that they did not find my commands grievous. When the father's business leads him much away, if a mother does not act with firmness and judgment, but waits until her husband comes home to complain, what will be the consequences to the poor children! It was his comfort to come home and have his little flock of well-ordered children running about his knees. When we were in town, the nice trays of cakes and buns, covered with clean cloths, used to be carried about the streets every afternoon, for sale. Although this would be shortly after our children's hearty dinner, they would get round their father and beg him to buy them some cakes. This he often did, and seldom less than half a dollar's worth would go round. I thought it a needless expense after they had dined, and remonstrated without much effect, but I sat down and calculated what the amount would be in a year for that not only unnecessary but hurtful luxury, leading the children to be gluttons and epicures, and one day, when they were about to call a cake woman, I said to Mr. Johnston, "Do you know what that amounts to in a year?" "No, Bess," was his reply. "Only

Recollections of a Georgia Loyalist

£26," I replied, which sum he never contemplated. He laughed and told the children that mother said cake cost too much money. I mention this to show the deference my husband paid to my opinions. These are by-gone days. Many bitter sorrows have I experienced in later years, but all for my good, I trust, as well as in punishment for my sins.

88

CHAPTER VI

WHEN my Eliza was seven years of age,
Mr. and Mrs. Wildman were about to
leave the island and settle in England, and
earnestly requested us to allow them to take
her as their own child, to educate. We could
not for some weeks make up our minds to
part with her, but after much reflection we
considered it best for the child, as she was
then of an age liable to the fevers of the
island and as most persons sent their children from Jamaica to school who had not
such good friends to entrust their children
to as we. So she went with them. Ann
Mackglashan also went under their care until
they arrived, when her grandfather and aunt
received her. My health now became worse,
my constitution much debilitated as the
result of ten years' residence in a warm climate, and the next year it was thought necessary that I should change climate. This I
was very averse to doing, as my husband
could not possibly leave his practice, and he

would not allow the children to be sent unless I went with them. It appeared a duty both to their health and their morals that they should not remain longer in the island, and after many days of painful anxiety, neither being able to give the sad fiat that separate we must, I did resolve with an aching heart, and embarked with my dear little family, for whom the sacrifice was made. Now, after forty years have elapsed, I can say with solemn truth that my own health alone would never have allowed me to leave my beloved husband and I should have risked the consequences of remaining. The ship *Roselle* for Leith was at Old Harbor, thirty miles from Kingston, where we were to embark, and on the morning of that sad day when I heard that the boat was come to take us on board (even now, when I remember my feelings I cannot refrain from grief) I hardly think I was in my senses. I uttered screams that distressed my poor husband to such a degree that he would then, I am convinced, have been glad if I had given up going. He begged me, if I felt so reluctant, to let him go on board and bring our things back, but all I could say was, "It is too late!" In the

midst of my distress I thought how incon-
sistent it would appear for me to stay, after
so much expense and trouble had been taken
in preparation, for though I may often have
been thought a vacillating creature, yet where
principle or character were concerned, I trust
I have been and can be firm. So the idea of
the good to my children prevailed, and I bore
the separation. My husband also felt it
keenly, for he loved his children and adored
his wife, but our separation was only to be
for one year or a little more.

The war still continued, and my son Andrew, then fifteen years of age, was dissuaded
by his Grandfather Johnston from going into
the navy, as he wished. The boy had even
already gone to Leith with some of his juve-
nile friends who had chosen that profession,
and had actually shipped on board a tender
which lay there; and it was with much difficulty that the Rev. Mr. Clive, a friend to
whose chapel Dr. Johnston and family went,
who had interest with the then regulating
captain at Leith, got him off. This was a
few weeks previous to my arrival in Edinburgh. Dr. Johnston had an idea that my
husband intended his son for the same pro-

fession as his own, and knew that he had it in his power to bring him forward in his practice. This being the case, and as he had no interest to bring him on in the navy, he induced Mr. Clive on my arrival to beg me to use my influence with my dear son to choose the medical profession. To our wishes his easiness of disposition and amiable, yielding temper led him to accede, but how much happier, in all human probability, would it have been for himself and his friends had he firmly adhered to his first choice. That want of firmness had been a marked feature of the child's character from very early infancy, and it proved ruinous to him in his subsequent life. In his early education many traits of character and little faults were kept by his too fond widowed aunt and her maiden sisters from his worthy old Grandfather Johnston's knowledge, which had he known he might have nipped in the bud. One day, when a little fellow, Andrew was with some companions near a stall in the High Street, filled with sugar candy, or "cut throat," as it is termed, and ginger cakes. The woman said to him, "Come, buy, laddie." He had no money, was his answer. "Give me your buttons," said the woman, and the poor foolish child allowed them to be cut off his coat. His aunts, so far as I could learn, neither punished him nor told his grandfather, and before long he went on to greater faults, which their ill-directed affection led them to pass over as well. With more watchful firmness over him he might have been made a sterling character, for his abilities were of a high order and his disposition was truly affectionate and amiable. In features he was remarkably handsome, and he stood six feet high and was well proportioned.

At last his father wrote to desire that he should be sent out to him that he might judge what he was best fitted for, and a few months after I arrived in Edinburgh he sailed from Leith for Kingston, Jamaica. His docility and quickness pleased his father, and he thought he would do credit to the medical profession, so eighteen months later he was sent back to commence a college course. Thus he was fixed in a profession which he did not fully like, and under the influence of several companions in Edinburgh, young men of fortune whom he had long known and to whom he was much attached, he was led often to neglect his classes and join in idle pleasures. Often of an evening he would order a fire in a separate room, with the fixed purpose of studying, when soon after he was quietly seated a rap would come at the door and he would be desired to be spoken with. Then the door would close and I would be told that Mr. Andrew and a gentleman had gone out. Thus my hopes of his reading for that night were frustrated, and I perhaps would not see him again until the next day. He was an excellent skater, and that robbed the lectures of many an hour's attendance. Yet so quick were his abilities that I have heard my valued friend, Dr. Thomas Duncan, who was most studious and who truly sympathized in my grief, say that he was astonished how much my son knew, though devoting so little time to his classes, or to study at home. Once Dr. Duncan wrote him a letter telling him how much I was afflicted, and saying that if he did not alter his conduct I would be forced to write his father, though dreading the effects of his displeasure and the grief and disappointment he would feel to have his fond hopes so dashed. Dr. Duncan so earnestly entreated him and begged for an interview, that for the time it melted his heart, and Andrew, having seen our friend, for a short time was all we wished. I had at last to write my husband, finding how dissipated a life Andrew was leading, and he, as soon as an answer could be received, desired him to be sent out to him. The poor fellow consented to go, though feeling the disgrace and misuse of talents that prevented his going with a diploma (a thing that was also bitterly felt by his father). Still, he was ever amiable, and in a letter I received from him on his way to Greenock, he feelingly wrote of the remorse he had at the pain he had given me, and said that he was often ready to throw himself on his knees before me and entreat me to forgive and forget his bad conduct, but that pride prevented. When he reached Jamaica he was received by, and for a while assisted, his father, yet I fear he never found that place in his father's heart he had once had. On his first residence in Jamaica he had the yellow fever, so fatal to new-comers. With unremitting care and with the blessing of Providence he got through it, however, and the second time he was there was very healthy. For four years and eight months before his death he was in practice with a medical man of high character, a Dr. Johnston (no relation of ours), a very liberal-minded man, who took my son into partnership with him in the mountains of Clarendon, and loved and valued him highly, and saw that his medical knowledge was good.

On Saturday, December 1, 1805, Andrew came with our friend and his very warm one, Mr. Hutchinson, to Kingston, with the intention of coming out to The Penn, our residence, three miles from Kingston, to see me and his sisters and his brother Lewis. We heard he was in Kingston, and expected to see him that evening, but he did not come, for he had a slight headache. His sisters, who dearly loved this affectionate brother, were eagerly looking for him, whose attentions to them were more like a lover's than a brother's. His father thought he should not have left his practice, and as there were races, thought that they had brought him; but I know differently. When his friend offered him a seat he could not resist the wish to see us and his father, who was on bad terms with him, which was a great grief to the poor boy, who was then doing well. The next day we were sure of seeing him. Alas, the servant who was sent in for marketing brought word he was not well. Still I had no idea of danger. His father had remained with him in town, and I had no means of getting to him, the only carriage we had, a chaise, the doctor having in town. To describe my anguish is impossible. What would I not have given to have seen him! Dr. Mackglashan called. I entreated him to take me to him, or to ask my husband to send for me. At three o'clock Mr. Johnston came. He said that Andrew had been taken with the black vomit, fatal symptom! in the night, and that his countenance indicated danger. He gradually sank, though tonics and brandy were given him largely, and he, dear child, did not, could not, bear to see our grief, and begged that we would not come.

At six o'clock in the evening Dr. Mackglashan came again. My three daughters were in the parlor. Poor Kitty had been a little better of her dreadful malady for some days, but was not told of her brother's danger. I again urged the doctor to take me, saying that anything was better than the state of suspense I was in. "Could you," he replied, "my dear Mrs. Johnston, submit if you knew the worst?" "Oh, yes!" I cried. "Your son died half an hour ago," was his heart-rending intelligence. As we stood together at the end of the balcony, I scarcely recollect how I felt, but this I know I uttered: "Shall we receive good at the hand of God and shall we not receive evil!" I then said, "I shall see his remains taken by this house." Even that was denied me. "No," he said, "you must be removed to my house, with the girls, in the morning, on Kitty's account, who might relapse, and you must not let either of the girls know of it to-night." Oh, what a hard trial for me! Yet I struggled until bedtime with my feelings, and was thankful to get to bed, so that I might give vent to my agonizing grief.

He sank calmly. Often have I thought what a comfort it would have been to me had he had a pious Christian minister or friend, even at the last, to have told him of his merciful Saviour. His father could not help saying (mentioning the calmness and quiet with which he left the world, and the smile that rested on his beautiful countenance) that he was sure there was no vice there. Would he had thought so long before! Less hardness would have had a better effect on his gentle nature. May that God that seeth not as man seeth, but who judgeth in mercy, have pardoned the errors of my ill-fated child, and have received him into glory, for He knoweth what man is, how frail and prone to sin! Our Heavenly Father sees and knows our hearts and will pardon where an earthly one will not.

Let this sad history of one cut off in the prime of life, at twenty-five years of age, with vigorous health, manly beauty (he was, as I have said, tall, well-proportioned, and with a face such as is seldom seen), be a warning to all my grandchildren to avoid idleness and dissolute companions, and to study in youth, that seed-time of knowledge, that they may reap the fruits of honest industry in after life and be an honor and credit to their parents. This dear child possessed every advantage of mind and person. He had abilities of the highest order, which he laid at the shrine of vice and folly, rendering his parents and friends miserable, his mother sorrowing the more that his father could not cordially overlook his past offences. My beloved offspring, to be sure of acting right, take the Bible for your guide, remember your Creator in the days of your youth, and pray that you may not be led into temptation. My poor son had false indulgence shown him in early life; even while at college his weak aunts rather took part against me, judging me too severe in wishing him to devote more of his time to study. I have had severe trials in this life, yet I am conscious that I deserved many, and none, I believe, have been more than was good for me. This is a long, sad history of my lamented first-born; let it be a warning to youth, and to parents to allow their sons to choose that profession their hearts most incline them to.

CHAPTER VII

IN the last chapter I digressed to give a full account of the termination of poor Andrew's earthly career. My son Lewis had been at an academy at Queen's Ferry and was well-principled and sedate, and his father wished him also to study medicine; accordingly, he wrote to Edinburgh to desire that he might attend some classes, and then go out to Jamaica previous to his ultimate study at college. After he got to Jamaica his mind turned to mercantile business, and his father got him into the office of a friend of his, a merchant of the first consequence, a Mr. Lake, where he remained four or five years, until 1806, with a salary of £200 per annum. Then he suddenly took a desire to study medicine, and was allowed by his father to go to Edinburgh. I remained in Edinburgh with my three daughters and two younger sons, my father residing with me, when the accounts from Jamaica of my husband's bad health led me to disregard what I most dreaded, a winter's passage in those Northern seas, and embark in the middle of November in the ship *Roselle*, at Leith, with my girls. I was at Dumfries with Laleah and Eliza on a visit to a friend when I got the letter, and I arranged with my friend Henry Duncan to take charge of my two dear boys, whom I was to leave behind. They were then to be boarded with a Mr. White at Dumfries, but were to be under his care, and I left my house furniture for my father to arrange, and parted from him and my two good little boys with a heavy heart. We had a long, rough passage of ten weeks, and encountered in the North Seas, some degrees beyond the Orkneys, where adverse winds had driven us, most tremendous gales.

While in this awful state my dear girls were calm and composed. My youngest, Laleah, then in her thirteenth year, who was on the same sofa with me, told me with some diffidence she had made some verses. As she had never before been visited by the Muses, it appeared strange at such a time to be inspired, the seas literally running mountains high. With much persuasion I got her to consent to allow a gentleman to write the

verses down, for we could not raise our heads.
I must transcribe them, as they show that
her mind had early been led to things that
are important, and that she was an affectionate and dutiful child:

> The warring elements obey
>   The Lord's Almighty power,
> The northern blast's by him controll'd
>   Even at this very hour.
>
> O why am I so much afraid,
>   Why does each wave alarm,
> Does not the Lord protect me still
>   And guard me by his arm?
>
> Then let me think I'm here as safe
>   As when in Scotia's Isle;
> A Mother's cheerful countenance
>   Makes all her children smile.

I observed, upon hearing the last verse, that
she might make some lines on her mother, and
to my wonder, an hour after she whispered
she had done so. These verses also were
taken down, and my heart feels too grateful
to my affectionate child, even after so many
years have rolled on, not to put them also in
these recollections of by-gone days, the retro-
spect of many of which, alas, is too, too
sad.

Recollections of a Georgia Loyalist

TO MY MOTHER.

How can I e'er repay the care
    That thou hast ta'en of me,
Or how restore the nights of rest
    I oft have stolen from thee ?

'Twas thou that taught my infant heart
    To raise itself in prayer,
The goodness of Almighty God
    Thou didst to me declare.

May every blessing light on thee
    To enrich thy mortal store,
And may the choicest gifts of Heaven
    Be thine for evermore !

We arrived safe and well the 1st of January, 1802, and I found my husband in bad health, but happy to meet us and much pleased with his three dear girls. Catharine, then nineteen, an agreeable, fine-looking woman, with a great flow of spirits and highly accomplished, had great quickness of intellect and ready wit, but a temper unequal, and subject to violent changes. Though she was five or six years older than her sisters, her judgment could not be relied on as much as that of either of them. From being considered a woman so long before they grew up she assumed toward them a haughty superiority, which she could not be brought wholly to lay aside when they went into company, and in this way she caused me much distress of mind. She selfishly desired many expensive articles, which the others quickly relinquished, knowing their father could not well afford them, and if she was opposed poor Catharine sometimes exhibited a temper that we had to take pains to prevent being made public.

These considerations caused me, weakly perhaps, it may be thought, to yield to her in many things. Had her Grandfather Johnston never taken her from me, thinking to benefit her by the advantages she would gain in Edinburgh, I should have controlled her temper, as I had hitherto done, and given her soberer views, and she would, like my other children, have been obedient to my will. She was only ten years of age when she left me, and four years passed before I joined her in Scotland, and a very different method of training from mine had been pursued with her by her aunts. They taught her the catechism, made her go to church, boxed her ears when she was wild and giddy, and allowed her free access to a circulating library, where nonsubscribers could for a penny get a novel for twenty-four hours. She was fond of reading, and with her quick intellect, had I been with her at first, before the poison took deep hold, could have become interested in studies of a higher kind. When she heard I was coming to Edinburgh, she imagined me like a heroine in a romance, and thought that I would be such a mother as was pictured in the highly wrought novels she was accustomed to read; while on the other hand, as soon as I arrived, her aunts loaded me with complaints of how foolish and giddy she was. Perhaps I was too anxious to counteract the faults that had been fostered so long, and may have tried to check them too suddenly. Though she saw the docility of her young sister Laleah, yet upon every attempt I made to alter her disposition she imputed to me a preference for her sister, which she thought caused my reproofs to her, and so a fatal jealousy sprang up in her mind. Little by little she brought herself into a highly nervous state, and as her health was beginning to decline from her irritability, we tried several changes for her. When we reached Jamaica she was in excellent health, and very much admired, for she was handsome and well made and was a proper height, and she played, sang, and danced admirably; yet her passions were strong and her judgment weak.

Soon after we arrived in Jamaica my dear Eliza took the yellow fever. A friend of Mr. Johnston, a Mr. Hutchinson, had kindly invited us to his residence, the Papine estate, six miles from Kingston, for the country air and to prevent infection in the hot town, and though we went, Eliza soon sickened. I sent an express off for her father immediately, who lost no time in coming. She had a little headache and languor, and only complained in the middle of the day, yet her father told me that evening that if she was not better in a few hours she could not recover. It did please God to restore her, and the others continuing in good health, six weeks after we removed to our own house near Halfwaytree. Mr. Johnston's health had been declining for some time, and it was now thought necessary that he should have change of climate, though it seemed hard for me after our long separation to be again tried in the same way. But so it was, and he was away two years, though unhappily he did not find much benefit from the change.

During his absence Laleah was attacked with yellow fever and was very ill. After his return Catharine was afflicted with a nervous illness, combined also with symptoms of yellow fever, and was seized with a violent bleeding at the nose, which nearly exhausted her. She got no rest, and was very irritable, and her father was persuaded by Dr. Mackglashan to give her an opiate, which he did, at the same time being aware that if it failed in its effects it would produce dreadful consequences. He gave her eighty drops of laudanum, and his worst fears were verified. It produced the most violent delirium, and she was in a dreadful state, thinking that there was an insurrection of the slaves, that they had set fire to the house, and that the bed she lay on was in flames and we were holding her in it. It took six persons to hold her in bed, and her poor father said to me that night that if she did recover from the violence and dreadful derangement she showed, he feared something fatal had taken place that would render her an idiot for life. After some days of delirium she sank into a state of insensibility, in which she remained three weeks without motion. Only by holding a glass to her lips could you tell she breathed, and indeed she was with great difficulty kept alive at all. The first sign of returning animation she showed was her shedding a few tears as a gentleman and lady who were fond of her, as she was of them, came into the room dressed in deep black. She was reduced to a skeleton, and for three months said no more than " Yes " or " No " when spoken to, but would scream if her father left her either night or day. Her dear sisters had not their clothes off for three months, and for eighteen did not go out into company. They were young in years, but well schooled in patience and self-denial. Doubtless the trial was of service ultimately in forming their characters and producing in them much sterling worth, though it was a fiery trial in the furnace of affliction. After a time Catharine was so much better that she could converse rationally. Then she told her sisters what she had suffered, how she had thought she was in flames and was being dragged over broken bottles. While she lay apparently insensible, she said, she imagined she was in a charnel house, where she was not permitted to move or speak. Such were the sufferings of my unhappy child. Slowly she continued to improve, and she sometimes appeared to take pleasure in the piano, which she had always been fond of and on which she formerly played and sang so well. Some months after, however, she relapsed into such a state of violence and irritation that a sea voyage was recommended, and worn down as I was with sorrow of various and trying kinds I told her father that as he could not leave his practice to go with her, hard as another separation from him and my beloved boys was, I myself would go. At once a vessel for New York was looked for, and my father, who was then on a visit to us, agreed to accompany me and my three daughters.

Not meeting a vessel quite suitable, a friend chancing to meet my husband said to him: "Why, Doctor, I wonder you who are a loyal subject do not prefer sending your family to a British Province; there is an excellent vessel going to Halifax, Nova Scotia." Little did I then think that I and all my children would ultimately settle in Nova Scotia.

Recollections of a Georgia Loyalist

When I heard this advice and knew that my father was looking at the accommodations of the Halifax vessel for us, so little intercourse had we with Halifax that I exclaimed, "Send us to Nova Scotia! What, to be frozen to death? Why, better send us to Nova Zembla or Greenland." So it was, however, and early in the summer of 1806 my father and three daughters with myself embarked in a brig of Prescott & Lawson's, for Halifax, perfect strangers to every one in that place except Mr. Thomson's family, who I had reason to think were not living in town, but at a place called Hamitfield, some distance away. Mrs. Thomson and I were both born and brought up in Savannah, and were schoolfellows there. I had a letter from a merchant in Kingston to Prescott & Lawson, and another to James and William Cochran, merchants. From the gentlemen and their wives to whom the first letter was addressed we met with much more than civility, they were as kind as near relations could have been. Mrs. William Lawson took us four females and my woman to her house, where we remained until I got a house and furnished it. Mr. Prescott took my father to his house, and with great kindness laid in our coal and potatoes and even marketed for us. Old Mr. and Mrs. Lawson were everything that was affectionate and kind, as were all the branches of their family. I found the Thomsons in Halifax, and I was very happy to meet my old friend after so long a separation.

My daughter Catharine for a time appeared to benefit from the change, and went a good deal into private company, and from her playing on the piano, which she did well, and her singing and conversation, she was the delight of all who heard her. But in a few weeks, when the novelty wore off and the effects of the sea air subsided, she relapsed into her former irritable state. I have great reason to think, however, that there was in her case more of temper and nervousness than real mental disease, though the latter did exist. Her condition was a source of much pain and many privations to myself and her dear sisters. Soon after our arrival in Halifax we met a friend of Mr. Grassie and the Messrs. Lawson, a Mr. Ritchie, a lawyer at Annapolis. He soon became attentive to my beloved daughter Eliza, and some time after made proposals to her. His character stand-

Sir William Johnstone Ritchie, K.C.B.
Late Chief Justice of Canada

ing high in the estimation of his friends and my daughter not objecting, her father was written to at Kingston, Jamaica, for his consent, which from the recommendations he received from several persons in Halifax was readily given. They were married at Halifax, June 30, 1807, and a few days after Mr. Ritchie took Eliza home, accompanied by her beloved sister Laleah, for they were tenderly attached to each other, being only fourteen months apart in age. Laleah remained at Annapolis until bad accounts of my dear husband's health, which called for my immediate departure, made me write for her. Then Mr. Ritchie kindly brought my dear Eliza also with her to stay with me until we sailed.

My good old father had been on a visit to Annapolis but had returned to Halifax, and he could not bring his mind to encounter a second time the climate of Jamaica, which did not agree with his health or habits of life, he being always accustomed to take much exercise on foot in cooler climates. Accordingly he decided to fix himself at Annapolis near his beloved granddaughter, to which decision I readily agreed for her sake as well as his, since then Eliza would not be left without one dear relative. As it was, the parting on both sides was severely felt. She was a dear, good child, and her heart was so affectionate, so free from self, that none ever knew her without loving her. At this moment, though more than seventeen years have passed since she was consigned to an early grave, I feel all the tenderness of grief as though it were very recent. My daughter Catharine had been much worse about the time of her sister's marriage, and afterward my troubles with her were great and sore, yet not more than my Heavenly Father thought was needful for me. I humbly pray that every chastisement may bring me more and more from loving the things of this world, and render me daily more patient under trials and disappointments of every kind.

CHAPTER VIII

THE 4th of December, 1807, we embarked on board the ship *Rosina* for Kingston, Jamaica, and had a good passage, except for a melancholy accident which happened to a passenger. A few hours after embarking a Miss Nancy Aikmann fell down the companion stairs against a trunk in the entry and broke her leg. Fortunately, however, we were near the *Muros*, our convoy, who sent her surgeon on board. The leg being much fractured, it was thought expedient to take it off, and that night by nine o'clock it was done. The sufferer bore the strain with unexampled fortitude. The assistant surgeon remained on board the whole passage, and the surgeon, Mr. Emwright, came frequently to help him. The latter was so charmed with Miss Aikmann's sweetness and cheerful patience, that after our arrival in Kingston he made her offers of marriage. No doubt her father's being a very rich man may have added one more charm in the eyes of the lover.   The couple were married some months later in England.

The 1st of January we arrived, and there soon after anchoring at Port Royal I had to meet the sad intelligence of my dear husband's death, he having passed away the 9th of December, 1807, three weeks before our arrival.   It was a bitter disappointment to me, as I had earnestly trusted we should meet again in life.   Dropsy, after a complication of diseases, was the final cause of his death.   We went up with our kind Captain Potter in his boat to Kingston, where a carriage met us to convey us to Mr. John Campbell's house.   He was a friend, and one of the trustees of my husband's estate.   Every soothing attention was shown us by Mr. and Mrs. Campbell, and soon after we got there my two dear sons, John and James, came to us, mingling their tears with ours—it was a sad meeting.   In the afternoon our good friend Dr. Mackglashan (also another trustee) came in and took us to The Penn, where I remained about a week, when I went to our own house at Halfwaytree.   The doctor was a true friend and did all the practice of the workhouse in Kingston for the widow and orphan daughters, so that the position could be kept until my son Lewis came out from Edinburgh. The physician of the workhouse was elected annually, yet my husband had held the post from the first, and he was now succeeded in it by my son. It was a lucrative position, though some months more so than others. Several months it paid between £80 and £90, none less than £40 or £50. Dr. Mackglashan attended the estates for the same object, to keep them for Lewis, and while he was absent he gave the emoluments of both the workhouse and the estates to me. The Mackglashans were the sincerest of friends, from Mrs. Mackglashan's first coming to Jamaica to the period when I finally quitted the island. They were with the doctor and myself as brother and sister; but they are now no more. I have outlived many of my contemporaries, and feel the departure of each one a loud call upon me, " Be ye also ready." The Rev. John Campbell, rector of St. Andrew's parish, was another trustee for my husband's estate. He and his family were much attached to me and my family, and were kind and benevolent in their dispositions. The Mackglashans are gone, and

Mr. and Mrs. Campbell have long since paid the debt of nature.

I remained in Jamaica three years before our affairs could be so settled as to admit of our leaving the island. The spring after my going there my son James went to Annapolis, Nova Scotia, to his brother-in-law and sister, who resided there. He lived with them until I went there, and it was a great comfort to his sister Eliza to have him with her. At the end of the year my son Lewis came from Edinburgh and commenced the practice of medicine in Kingston, and the January after he was duly elected to the attendance of the workhouse there. My other son John was with Mr. Munro in the office, and had a salary of £200 per annum, Jamaica currency. His character from early life was good and dutiful, and he was strict in his principles. When he came out from Scotland from under the care of his excellent friend and tutor, Duncan, at the age of fifteen, he evinced a strength of character seldom observed in one so young. A friend of mine who was at the head of one of the largest law offices in Kingston, a Mr. Munro, offered as a favor to take him into his office. At that time it was the shocking custom in the law offices to have clerks at the office on Sunday mornings until twelve o'clock. It was then too late to attend divine service, which as in other places began at eleven o'clock. When I told my beloved John of Mr. Munro's offer and asked if he had any objection to the profession, he said he had none, but at the same time he requested that I would ask that his Sundays should be passed as he had been used from childhood to pass them; that he should not be compelled to be at the office on Sundays at all. When I told Mr. Munro his request, he asked me if John would attend church. "Certainly; it has ever been his custom to do so," was my reply. He then promised me he would grant his request, but no other except the head clerk, Mr. Marshall, had the same privilege. Mr. Marshall was a pious young man, very useful in the office, and as might be expected from one of his good principles, very faithful. His salary was £500 per annum. My dear boy was also most conscientious, and went almost an hour earlier than the other clerks and left the latest, so he well made up the time of the few hours on the Sabbath, which he could not answer to his Divine Master to break.

Some years after, an elderly friend, who was about putting his son into the same office, told me that Mr. Munro had said to him that no one except the head clerk should be exempt from Sunday attendance. I told my friend the promise had been given my boy and I could not think it would be broken. Should it be so, I hoped my child would be able to earn his living some other way, without breaking the divine law, and added that I had never prayed for riches for my children, but rather that they should be good, religious members of society. "After all, Dr. M——," I added, "they can only starve, and though that would be a lingering death it would be better than sinning against their consciences." When my dear John came home I told him what had passed, and asked if Mr. Munro had said anything to him on the subject. He answered he had not, but should he do so his mind was made up. When anything agitated his calm mind he became very animated, and on that occasion he took many rapid strides across the room, at the same time saying he was resolved not to remain; but he was never spoken to on the subject. My friend was balanced between the feelings of a man of the world and the breaking of a commandment, and he no doubt hoped to have my son keep his poor son in countenance. To the office his son went, and from mercenary motives became an habitual Sabbath-breaker. The poor lad had been religiously brought up in England under the eye of a pious aunt, whose heart ached at the sad alternative. Alas, what sacrifices are daily made at the shrine of Mammon, and how little pains are taken to secure that inheritance that fadeth not away!

CHAPTER IX

AS I have already said, it was nearly three years from my return to Jamaica before I could get the affairs of the estate so arranged by the trustees as to allow of my return and that of my two daughters, Catharine and Laleah, to Nova Scotia. In the summer of 1810 we embarked for Halifax, accompanied by my son John, whose health required a few months' change of climate, and who had obtained leave from Mr. Munro to remain as long as he felt it necessary. On my arrival at Halifax we were kindly received by all our friends there, and not long after Mr. Ritchie came to town with his horse and gig to take us to Annapolis. Catharine and myself went with him in his carriage, and another horse and gig were hired for dear John and Laleah. We arrived safely at Annapolis, where we had the happiness of meeting my father, my beloved Eliza, and my son James, who had left me the year before. My Eliza had two dear boys. John was two and a half years old, Thomas, a stout boy, ten months old. Their mother was looking thin, but well in spirits, the fatigue of nursing and having the charge and attendance of two such children, without a regular servant, was more than a delicate female brought up as she had been was equal to. As soon as I went to housekeeping I relieved her of part of her care by having John stay with us. We helped Eliza, especially on wash day, a grand event which occurred once a fortnight in every family, at which all the servants assisted, and when it was thought a great indulgence if the mistress had no more labor than to have the fag of all the children. These customs were new to my beloved child, brought up as she had been in the habits and comforts of a lady, who had had that and other work done by servants, all with their regular employments. On those stirring days I had Tom also brought to my house, who if he was not quite as great a favorite with his grandfather as his first great-grandson John, who bore his name, was with his Aunt Laleah and myself a great pet. Mr. Ritchie's mother had the charge of his house and took the head of his table; she was old, but well and active, and would have felt the want of her usual employments had dear Eliza as mistress of the house taken the sole management upon herself. She, however, had enough to occupy her, with a rapidly increasing family and the care of nursing and attending upon them. She was an affectionate wife, and a tender and judicious mother, and she was a great economist. In her lively manner she used to say, when we laughed at her for putting together as many as ten pieces from a pair of her husband's trousers to make a suit of clothes for little Johnny: "While Ritchie has to work so closely in his office, I think it my duty to save all I can." That spirit of pride, or ambition shall I term it, that led her to try how much butter she could herself make in a season, was more than her delicate frame could long endure. Besides, her rest was always liable to be broken by an infant at night. Until John was past three years of age, however, he lived with me, and from an old-fashioned prayer-book with large print I taught him his letters and to spell little words. I think he will now be glad to find that I wish him to accept the sacred book, and leave it for him to remember his old grandmother and dear aged great-grand-father by, who so greatly doted on him. The book may be valued, too, for its antiquity, it having been printed in Queen Anne's reign. If he has children he may say, "This was your great-grandmother's."

My dear Eliza had dear Laleah added to her family January 16, 1812. Her next was William Johnston, born October 29, 1813. My beloved father died the 4th of November after—making just one week between the birth of the infant and the demise of the aged great-grandparent. He had a rapid dropsy, which was tapped with apparent success, but in a few days the water increased greatly and he went off very suddenly. At his request, I had left him for a few moments sitting up in the arm-chair, for he had been better that day and had conversed a little with me. I could not stay long away, however, fearing he might feel weak if he rose from the chair, and I called at the door, "Allow me to come in now?" There was no answer, and I went in just in time to save him from falling off the side of the bed where he was, against the edge of the hard bedstead. He was then very faint, and just as I approached fell back on the bed. I was alone. He was a heavy man, his legs were hanging over the bed and he was in danger of falling, but I got on the bed, raised him in my arms, and strength was given me to support him from slipping down. His dear, venerable head lay on my shoulder, he breathing quick, but gently as an infant. There was no creature in the house at the time but my poor daughter Catharine, and I screamed for her. She came to me, and I begged her to fly to Mrs. Fraser, and bring her, Dr. Hinckle, or anybody. She went, and Mrs. Fraser and Dr. Hinckle both came in, and took my beloved parent from my arms and laid him on the pillow, when with two gentle breathings he was gone. Mr. Ritchie and Dr. Robertson, who were at the Court House, soon came and helped me to my chamber, where I lay completely exhausted after my exertion of mind and body.

My dear Laleah, who had been the tenderest of nurses for weeks, and was ever, as were all my children, the most dutiful and affectionate of grandchildren, seeing him so much better that morning, told me that if I sat with my father she would go and see her sister and get a little fresh air, and also, chief of her errand, get some eggs to clear jelly for her grandfather, little thinking how soon he was to be called away. He was a fond parent, and thought only too much of his child and her offspring. I hoped I had done my duty but, alas! what child can say, when deprived of a beloved parent, that she has not been wanting in numberless instances whereby she could have shown her love and gratitude.

My beloved Eliza before her confinement was daily with us, helping to take care of her dear grandfather, and feeling that every day would be the last she could expect to keep up. The last day, October 28th, she said: "I will stay as long as I can, for I know I shall not in all likelihood see him again," and she remained until ten o'clock that night. The next morning we heard that her little son William was born. My son James arrived that morning from Halifax, and as soon as my dear father saw him, he said, " You have come, my child, to see one just come into the world and another about quitting it." All who knew the dear old gentleman revered and loved him. He was in his seventy-ninth year, and I, his only child, now recording these events, am past since May last my seventy-second year. But what avails the longest life? It is but as a vapor, so soon passeth it away. "So teach me to number my days that I may apply my heart unto wisdom."

My dear Laleah was married, January 29, 1814, after these events, to Dr. William Almon, and I trust the union has been a happy one. Religion, I mean vital religion, was then at a low ebb, but he was brought up by parents who were regular in their duties and attentive to the morals and religious observances of their children. Great changes have taken place in Halifax since that period, and low as is still the standard of Christianity among the bulk of the community, yet many souls have lately been awakened to see their need of a Saviour's atoning blood, and to rejoice that His free grace can wash them from all their sins if they only have faith in Him. We must all who are concerned in these momentous questions pray that Christ's kingdom may daily be extended over our land, and that our children may be rescued from the dominion of Satan.

Recollections of a Georgia Loyalist

On November 20, 1814, their first child was born, a daughter, who was called Laleah. January 27, 1816, their son William Johnston was born. February 9, 1816, my daughter Eliza's son, James Johnston, was born. He was called after his Uncle James, who was also his godfather, which at that time met his wishes. Elizabeth Lightenstone Ritchie was born October 1, 1817, and my daughter Laleah's dear Amelia was born July 20, 1817. Our beloved and ever-to-be-lamented Eliza soon after got a typhus fever, which injured her constitution, and she was in delicate health for some time. I left Annapolis when her child was three weeks old, and passed the winter in Halifax with my daughter Laleah, but returned to Annapolis in the spring. Myself and all her family were very anxious that our dear Eliza should be taken to another climate, but our entreaties did not prevail and that summer passed away and she was still ailing and weak.

The winter of 1819 found her growing worse; a short cough, hectic flush, and feverish symptoms gave us real cause for dread, and all that winter she was confined between her bedroom and the drawing-room on the same floor. Dear James and Bessy were her constant companions. I also saw her almost daily, no weather keeping me from her. My son James drove his sister Laleah up in May to see their beloved Eliza, and she brought her youngest babe, whom she was nursing, with her. She was called Elizabeth, after me. Our dear invalid rallied a little and was downstairs a few times to dinner, but soon after kept chiefly upstairs. She expected to be confined early in June. James and Laleah could not remain so long, and they parted for ever (at least in this world) from their dear and most beloved sister. She, too, must have had a presentiment that her continuance would be short, by her wishing and proposing that her sister should take her daughter Laleah with her, that at her death she might be brought up by that darling sister whom from infancy she had loved as her own soul. This we conjectured could be her only motive for parting from her child at such a time. After they were gone she often begged me to request her sister to get her Laleah improved in writing, that she might write her often, and she frequently spoke of it. Whether her Laleah made out a line to her mother I do not remember. She seemed to feel the parting from her, as she was seven years and a half old, and a very companionable child.

On the 14th of June of this, to me, eventful year Mr. Ritchie came in the morning to break the news to me of the death of my dear daughter Catharine, which took place on the 2d of June. It was a shock to me, as I had formed the plan, if dear Eliza recovered from her confinement, to go to Boston to see her. If I found her well enough in mind I intended to bring her home. My son John was to visit us that summer, and what hopes, what happiness were anticipated in such a meeting of dear friends. Alas, my Heavenly Father in His wisdom saw fit to order it far otherwise, and to frustrate our earthly schemes. On the day that I heard of poor Catharine's death I could not venture to see Eliza, lest I should by look or feeling discover the sad news to her. Dear creature, ever mindful of her mother's comfort, and suspecting that I would not eat any fruit or other nice thing I got but keep it until hers were done, that day got some oranges from her brother James, who wrote her he had sent her a larger supply by a vessel. She gave Mr. Ritchie's niece Harriet Ritchie some oranges to take to me, with strict charges to be sure to cut some of them and see that I ate a part, so thoughtful was she ever for the comfort of others, especially of her mother. If I were called upon to bear testimony whose individual character I had ever known most free from selfishness, I could with truth and boldness say it was my beloved Eliza's. In early childhood she evinced the disposition to impart to others whatever she had, and the disposition grew with her growth.

That night she was seized with violent fever, and it was thought had taken cold from imprudently cutting out a piece of Russia sheeting, which might have had a cold dampness about it. Be that as it may, she continued ill all night, and next day labor came on, and in the evening (June 15) dear George was born. She was put to bed that night extremely weak, but she thought herself better and slept a few hours very comfortably. When she awoke she observed that she had not enjoyed so much good sleep for a long time. After that, however, she was not so well. Dr. Randolph had been called away to another female patient and did not see her, but early next day, when he did, he was much alarmed at her situation. She had great pain in her chest and oppression of breathing, and he advised bleeding, and wished to call in Dr. Simpson. I was in agonies to have Mr. Ritchie send express to Kentville for Dr. Bayard, and he had the horse and his faithful man Quin ready to start, when the doctor said to Mr. Ritchie he thought he had better defer sending until they saw the effects of the bleeding. He yielded, poor man, and I was sadly distressed, for though that was Wednesday night, the doctor could not possibly have got there, using all the haste he might, before Friday night.

It was the will of God. When He is about to call us hence there are many ways of ordering events, which our poor, blind, ignorant minds cannot discern. Submission is our part, yet how hard a lesson it is for most of us to learn.

On Wednesday evening she was bled, but though sensible the first two days after her delivery, she never got any better, and it appeared that she apprehended danger, for upon their bringing her a night-cap to change, she observed that it was one of her best and that the vinegar used about her head might spoil it and she wanted another. When Miss Cross was trying to make the infant take the breast, which he was long doing, Miss Cross said: "Take it, you little fooly." My sweet Eliza smiled, and in her playful way said, "That's not a family failing, Margaret." From Thursday she grew worse, wandered a good deal, and often repeated, "What does it avail, what does it avail!" Once when I was standing by her bedside she repeated these words, "My children, my poor children!" I asked what she wished for them, but she seemed to have gone off from the subject. The post was going, and I wrote my dear James and also Dr. Bayard, to hasten their coming. But it was too late for any human skill to avail. She soon sank into a stupor, and on Saturday afternoon, the 19th of June, 1819, departed this life, after a short mortal struggle, leaving all who had ever known her to deplore deeply her loss. She was only in her thirty-second year, and so was cut off in her prime. Our Heavenly

Father, in thus early removing my beloved child, no doubt saw in His infinite wisdom that it was best for her, yet we cannot see things as we ought, and it seems to us that it might have been better for her motherless children had she been spared. May the prayer that has been so often and fervently offered for these children at the throne of grace have been heard, and may they be blessed with all needful temporal good, and above all with the grace that may lead each one to supplicate at the throne of grace for a renovation of heart!

Dr. Bayard and my dear James rode day and night, and arrived on Tuesday night at ten o'clock, and no words can describe the grief of my son, who had not realized her danger, to find his sister a corpse. We had kept her remains with difficulty, in the hope that he would be in time to attend the last solemn offices, and this he was enabled to do. On Wednesday morning her dear remains were interred in the Annapolis churchyard, where my dear father lies, and where dear Laura was laid some years since and an infant child who was still-born. It is a place hallowed to me, and I could wish my remains might rest in the same spot; but there is little chance of that happening, as I am now in Halifax, and from my age it is not likely I shall ever pay Annapolis another visit.

After these heavy losses, the anticipated pleasures of that expected summer were overthrown to us survivors. My dearest son John went to New York, intending to visit Boston on his way, that he might see his sister Catharine. When he arrived there he found that she had departed this life a week before. It was no doubt a shock and disappointment to him, yet not one to cause such poignant grief as he was soon after to feel, for Catharine's had been for years a life of suffering and mental disease, with no chance of recovery, and she was now released from its continuance. John soon left Boston for Annapolis, where he arrived a few days after the funeral of our dear Eliza, and where he remained a few months with us.

I soon broke up housekeeping to live with Mr. Ritchie and watch over his children's health and morals. I stood to them now in the place of their dear mother, for I knew well her wishes, plans, and hopes for her children. Her great principle was to exact from them

Recollections of a Georgia Loyalist

implicit obedience, and those who were old enough at her death evinced by their conduct the benefit they derived from her discipline. After awhile my dear John went to Halifax to see his sister Mrs. William Almon and her family, and his brother James, who resided there and practised as a barrister. Some time after he returned to Annapolis to see us, and then, about January 7, 1820, he went back to Jamaica.

CHAPTER X

ONE evening I received a letter from my dear James, announcing as carefully as he could his intention of going to Madeira for his health. He was going, he said, merely to please his friends, and I must not suppose there was any cause for alarm, for he was not very unwell. It was thought, he said, that escaping the winter would establish his health perfectly. He wrote everything that such an affectionate child would be sure to write, to reconcile me to the dread of what might happen, but after so recently losing my beloved Eliza, his determination fell upon my spirits that night most heavily. At length I betook myself to my only source of consolation, and on my knees prayed at the throne of grace for my child's safety, and then opened the Word of Life. Let it not be called enthusiasm when I say that my eyes lighted on some most consoling texts of Scripture, which did then and after strengthen and comfort me. I felt assured my child would be

138

preserved, and I rose with a firm trust that my prayer was heard. From that time I was peaceful, and although the day after he sailed, the 1st of February, there was a heavy snow storm and gale, still I knew in whom I trusted and was not cast down. My dear John, the morning after James' letter came, set out on horseback to see his brother. He also was going back to Jamaica, and this event hurried him off sooner than he would otherwise have gone; then he, too, parted from me. Mr. Edward Cutler accompanied him to Halifax, and his presence made the journey less dreary to him. It was hard to part with dear John, though he was then in good health. James arrived safely at Madeira, remained there a month, and returned after three months' absence, in good health, which filled my heart with gratitude to Almighty God, who had been so merciful to me. The cataract on my left eye now became gradually worse, until at length it obscured the sight, and not long after the other eye inflamed, and a cataract was just discernible in an incipient state. Through the use of medicines, however, it was suspended for a time, but at last my sight was almost obscured.

Recollections of a Georgia Loyalist

In the year 1821 my son James married Miss Amelia Almon, an amiable and well-principled girl, who, by her tender affection and religious, well-directed mind, has rendered him very happy. They have had a large family, of whom six are now alive, a seventh being expected shortly. My son Lewis removed to this country from Jamaica with his family about May, 1822, and settled in Halifax. He and his wife had then three daughters, but now their children number fourteen. By the mercy of our Heavenly Father they will, I trust, very soon be the happy parents of their fifteenth child. One they lost in Jamaica, a girl, Mary Ann, and another seven years and a half past, called William, a fine boy about three years of age. May a blessing be upon all my dear grandchildren, that they may be led to love religion and remember their Creator in the days of their youth! How happy was the good Philip Henry (Matthew Henry's father), whose children took religious, pious partners. Of the religious state of his twenty-four grandchildren he thought so well as to venture to say he thought "God had set His seal upon them." May we not humbly suppose that as his children married pious helpmates, the parents united in care and vigilance to infuse into their children's minds from early age the spirit of love to God and duty to men, and with earnest prayer sought a blessing on their endeavors. How much do I now see the necessity of forming religious connections, to insure comfort and joy to people's offspring. Yet, alas! how little is religion attended to even by religious parents, and still less by the young persons themselves.

When my sight failed I was very desirous to have something done to restore it if possible, and at one time I was advised to give an oculist from Boston a sum of money to come to Halifax, and pay all his expenses until his return. Indeed, my son Lewis came to Annapolis in June, 1823, to take me to Halifax for that purpose, but I ever felt reluctant to the plan, and Dr. Almon, with an eminent army surgeon, examined my eyes and I think put belladonna on them. The doctors found that the nerve was perfect, and that they were in good condition for an operation, but Dr. Almon, not seeming to think that the doctor from the States could do it better than our own medical men, entered into what had

been ever my own strongest wish, to go to
Scotland or England to the fountain head.
There was some difficulty for a time as to
who would go with me, but my mind was
made up to go, and I arranged with my
friends the Davidsons that I should go to
Edinburgh to them, and that Miss Davidson
would attend me to London and remain with
me until I was ready to go back with her to
Scotland, where I had a pressing invitation
to stay with her family a twelvemonth or
more. These were the husband and children
of my departed friend. However, my son
Lewis made up his mind to go himself with
me, and we embarked in the *Lady Wellington*
packet, the 20th of April, 1824, for Falmouth. We had a short but severe passage
and were nearly lost, the vessel being thrown
on her beam ends in the effort to lay her to.
We remained lying to for forty-eight hours,
the waves breaking over us all the time, but
it pleased the Lord to spare us. I was very
weak and worn out with the roughness of
the passage when I landed at Falmouth, but
I went on soon after to London, and was recommended to Mr. Lawrence, a celebrated
surgeon and oculist, who was also at the head

of the Eye Infirmary and gave lectures there to students. After much inquiry as to who was best, and after some weeks of preparation to bring my system to a more healthful state, he was fixed on, and on the 16th of June I was operated on in my left eye, and but for a faintness coming on after it, should then have had the other eye done also. Twelve days after, the right eye was operated on, but not with the same success; inflammation ensued and I suffered much from it for weeks, and became reduced and feeble. After all my suffering I have now no sight in it, but I do not regret that, since my sight is so mercifully restored in the other eye, which has since been free from weakness or inflammation. It is now thirteen years, or will be in June, since I received my sight, and for the blessing I can never be grateful enough to my Heavenly Father, who though He chastens yet in mercy gives comfort to His afflicted children.

Before I left England I was kindly invited by Mr. and Mrs. Brimmer Belcher to pass a week at their residence at Roehampton, a pleasant spot quite like the country, with lawn and gardens and greenhouse plants.

Recollections of a Georgia Loyalist

Lord Ellenboro, who was their landlord, lived within three-quarters of a mile of Clarence Lodge, where Mr. and Mrs. Belcher, Sr., resided; there I was also hospitably invited. After spending a week with the younger Belchers, I left, having experienced from Brimmer and his truly excellent wife the kindness and attention of children. I felt the more grateful as in my then weak state I was too ill to converse or afford them any pleasure from my company. At Clarence Lodge I stayed a month or more, and under Providence I think I owe to Mrs. Belcher and her kind-hearted family much of my recovery. I had together with good nursing every luxury that their then ample means afforded; it was the season when fruits of the greatest variety were in profusion, and they gave me these and indeed every other luxury that could be had, and all with the most affectionate kindness. I got my strength there, and returned to my lodgings quite recovered.

A few days before we were finally to leave London for Falmouth Mrs. Belcher took me in her carriage on a Saturday to Clarence Lodge, where I remained until Monday, when she returned to town with me. She gave me to take to sea a large basket of the nicest gingerbread, six bottles of very old Madeira, with a present of a handsome lace pelerine, and all appeared to take an interest in me. My gratitude to them will ever remain warm and sincere. I had a kind invitation from the Roupells to pass a few weeks with them at their country seat, twenty-eight miles from London on the way to Brighton, but Lewis was anxious to return to his family in Nova Scotia and he could not accept their kind invitation nor comply with the wish of Mrs. Johnston (wife of Judge Johnston of Trinidad) to take lodgings with or near her at a watering or sea-bathing place in Kent, where she was going for some weeks. No doubt these changes might have been of service to my health and have strengthened me more for my voyage a month after, but the reasons for sailing for home were strong with my son, and though my last treated eye was still weak and inflamed and I was not strong in body, yet it was so ordered that we left London on the 1st of September, 1824, for Falmouth, in a post-chaise. I had with me Sally Bower, my woman, and we slept that night at

Salisbury, the next night at Exeter (weather very hot indeed), and the next at Bodmin, and got to Silly's Green Bank Hotel next day, where we remained a few days. Lady Mitchell and her daughter, with Miss Uniacke and her brother Mr. James Uniacke, came down the day after us and were at the same hotel. They called on me at my apartments, and were very polite and civil. We were to be fellow-passengers in the same packet, and on the 9th we embarked, I going on board with Lady Mitchell in Captain King's barge, which he sent to take her and her family on board the *Cygnet*. The lieutenant and commander, Mr. Goodwin, was very attentive and obliging, and the accommodations were very comfortable and the fare excellent.

There was a Mr. Fraser on board, a civil engineer, going to Upper Canada with his newly-married wife. She was a very pretty looking, lady-like woman. Both were Scotch. She had been well-educated, and this was her first separation from indulgent parents and kind friends. She and her husband had been only three months married, and the poor lady was dreadfully homesick besides being very seasick; she was so ill the whole passage as never to be able to sit at a single meal, and she seldom even came on deck. She was unused to the sea and did not seem to know in any way how to remedy the evils she labored under, so with my usual wish to aid those who require it (Mr. Ritchie would call it Quixotism) I lectured the steward's mate, made him more attentive to her stateroom comforts, made her take good chicken broth and arrowroot at night with cheese and porter at times, got her into my cabin, which was more airy than hers, and was soon repaid by seeing her grow much better in health and spirits. She was very interesting. I had one letter from her from Upper Canada, and she appeared to estimate my trifling services much beyond their worth.

We arrived at Halifax the 13th of October, 1824, and found all well. I forgot to mention that while at sea my eye inflamed very much, and when I landed my children were disappointed and feared all my expense and exertion would prove useless. It pleased my Heavenly Father, who orders all things wisely, however, though I lost the sight of my right eye from inflammation, to preserve the other, and it has continued ever since healthy and strong. For this blessing I can never be sufficiently thankful. I recovered my health and strength in a few weeks, and remained at Dr. Almon's until May, 1825, when I heard of the death of Mrs. Ritchie. This induced me to go up immediately to Mr. Ritchie and his children and offer my services and consolation, and once more assume the care of my sweet Bess, who before her father's marriage had been long under my care, the child of my old days. My son John, who married in Jamaica, also came with his wife and settled in Annapolis, and while their house was repairing they visited Mr. Ritchie. My new daughter, dear Laura, was a charming young woman, the meekest and purest-minded being I have ever met with, from her spiritual-mindedness in religion appearing fitter for heaven than earth. Her first child, a fine girl, was still-born, for her sufferings were so long and protracted that the poor babe died just as it entered this world. The mother bore her sufferings with the patience of a saint. My beloved son had been persuaded to pass the night at Judge Ritchie's, and coming home early, finding his wife still suffering and danger apprehended, he fell down in the parlor in a swoon, which greatly alarmed me. Dear Laura had a better recovery than we could have hoped for, and about a year after she had a sweet little girl born, whom they called Mary.

Before her birth I removed to Halifax. Soon John and Laura came on a visit, with Mary, who was then eight months old and had a beautiful, angelic countenance, and sweet, winning ways. Alas, I fear she was too much an idol with both parents. When John was about to leave Annapolis to attend the House of Assembly at Halifax in the winter, he wished to bring his wife, and she also wished to accompany him, but the fear of risking their child's health in a winter journey (though she might have been guarded in a close-covered sleigh) made my son feel it best that dear Laura should remain at home with Mary, which she as usual meekly assented to. She was alone with two servant women and a boy, but as there were only a few that had minds congenial with her own, and as they could not for a time be with her, she preferred remaining as she was. The session was nearly over, a week more and her husband would again be with her. The first of April, in excellent health and spirits she wrote her husband a letter, her child being within a week of one year old. The stage was to leave next morning. Oh, shall I proceed! for even now after the lapse of eight years my heart sickens at the recollection. That night after reading and praying with her household, she retired to her own room, where she was wont to offer up her private devotions and read the Word of God to herself. The person who attended the child had laid her in bed, had seen that everything was right and that her mistress had no further commands for her, and had gone to the kitchen, which was next her room. Scarcely had she seated herself in the kitchen when she heard two knocks on the wall. She quickly hastened to the room, where she found Laura in a flame of fire. Another servant ran into the kitchen, where two buckets of water stood, and dashed water over her. But alas! everything on her was burned. Her body was fearfully burned, and she was an agonizing spectacle. A servant was sent for the doctor and for Mrs. Davies, a kind friend, and blankets were put over her for

she was then shivering. The words she uttered were: "This is a judgment of God's
to bring me nearer to Him," and at another
time: "Vanity of vanities, all is vanity!"
Everything was done by the doctor and
her friends to mitigate her pain, and what
medicine was best for her was given her.
She was wonderfully patient and calm, and
gave what account she could of the accident. She went to snuff her candle, and she
thinks the snuff fell on her clothes. My poor
child had that day for the first time laid off
her merino dress and put on a muslin one
with a deep flounce. It is thought that
in attempting to light her candle she may
have turned hastily round and her flounce
caught in the flame, for when she discovered
it the lower part of her dress was all on fire.
Her clothes were all loosened except the top
button of her frock, which she thought of un-
buttoning and letting drop off her with the
rest of her clothes, but her too nice modesty
shrank from this. Her next idea was to wrap
herself in the merino curtains of her bedstead, but she feared that she would set fire
to the curtains and risk the baby's life. Her
third was to take a pitcher of water and throw

over herself. I do not recollect whether all these thoughts passed through her mind before she knocked or not, but she had never been called upon to act for herself and had always had a governess, a parent, or a husband to look to for everything. Had it been otherwise, had she been trained to think and act for herself, she would have resorted to one of these means at the first appearance of the fire. Hers was a strong mind in matters that concerned her spiritual welfare, but in temporal things her diffidence led her to lean on others. It was the will of God. He saw that her pure and gentle spirit was fitter for mansions of bliss than to encounter the storms of adversity here, and the next morning she gradually sank into a stupor, and at 9 o'clock Friday night, April 2d, breathed her last. Thus was my meek, angelic child translated by a painful and sudden death into the presence of her Saviour and her God, where all is praise and adoration.

The sad news of the accident was carried to Halifax by William Ritchie, early on Friday morning. By his exertions he prevailed on the passengers to allow the stage to go off at 2 o'clock in the morning. When he got

to Kentville, where the stage was to stop,
the dear fellow hired a wagon and travelled
all night. The roads at that season were
deep and heavy, and he got to town only
about 10 o'clock Saturday morning, bringing a letter from Dr. Bayard telling my
son what had happened. He saw his poor
uncle in the street on his way to the House
of Assembly and had not the heart to tell
him, but when he asked how all were, contrived to evade the question by saying
he had a letter and would call with it.
My dear son was in a hurry to get to the
House of Assembly and William came immediately to his Uncle James', where I then
resided, and told him the dreadful news. He
went for my son Dr. Lewis Johnston, to accompany his poor brother to Annapolis and
take whatever was needful for the suffering
patient; then he went to the stage office and
engaged a wagon to go off directly. Next,
he called his uncle from the House and gave
him Dr. Bayard's letter, and he and Lewis
set out on their journey on Saturday forenoon,
the 3d of April. The roads were so bad that
with their utmost exertion they did not reach
Bridgetown until early Monday morning, and

there they heard of Laura's death. The shock to his nervous system, added to the fatigue of his journey and the exhaustion of his winter's work, threw my son into an alarming state, and he went at once into a kind of fit. Fortunately, however, his brother was with him to use means for his recovery, and they got to Annapolis the day before the funeral.

Laura's face had escaped disfigurement, which was a comfort to all her friends, but from dear Lewis' account of the rest of her body it was dreadful to behold. O how mysterious and past the conception of finite creatures are the ways of God; they are past finding out, yet all is done in wisdom and mercy. We can only wonder, adore, submit, and kiss the rod, praying for that divine aid which may, indeed, enable us to say, "Thy will, not mine, be done."

CHAPTER XI

I WENT to Annapolis as soon as the roads were passable, and remained with my son and took care of sweet little Mary, who was more than ever an idol with her only parent. She was certainly a lovely child, with a most amiable disposition, which has always continued with her. Some years after, my age and his anxiety about his dear child induced my son again to think of marriage. What was at first suggested to him by motives of friendship and prudence was by and by urged upon him by stronger feelings. Meeting unexpectedly with a pleasing, amiable young lady, a Miss Kelly, whose character he had heard highly extolled, his heart was soon wholly hers, and he was not long in declaring himself. She also had heard by their mutual friends the Bayards of St. John his character highly praised; and indeed they knew so much of each other from different people that when they first met they were far from being really strangers. They were married the 17th of

155

September, 1832, and lived happily together for the few years it pleased God to spare my son. They had a daughter, a fine child, whom they called Laura after his former wife, and sixteen months after her birth they had a son, called James Kelly, after his maternal grandfather.

My beloved son always enjoyed good health, and he came up to Annapolis (where I was then on a visit) to attend the September Court. After the Court was over he hurried down to Clare to visit his constituents in that part of the county, and when he returned was in Wilmot also for the same purpose. On Saturday he left Annapolis for Kentville by the stage, a conveyance which often makes travelling very rough and severe. He must have felt it so, from his writing me from Kentville by no means to come in that coach for it would be too much for me. My beloved child was ever mindful of his mother's comfort. He went on Monday in the other stage that travels from Kentville to Halifax, but stopped at Mrs. Fultz's, where his wife and family were, for change of air, and a day or two later they all returned to town together. A few days after they reached Halifax he ruptured a blood vessel, but it was not then thought certain whether the blood he discharged was from his lungs or from some of the vessels in the back of the throat. I returned from Annapolis soon after, and was greatly shocked to find how ill he had been and how weak and pale he still was. After that he never wholly recovered his health and strength, and he often had colds and coughs.

At last he was advised to go immediately to the West Indies. It was then, however, November, and the winter setting in severe he did not go. When the House of Assembly met in January his medical and other friends urged upon him the necessity of not attending the session. My dear child would attend, however, and though promising he would not stay many hours at a time in the House, when he was once there he got too much engaged in what was doing to adhere to his resolution. Indeed, I never knew him enter so much into the spirit of what was doing in the legislature as that winter. For a time he used to write late every night on the currency question, a labour which was fatiguing to both mind and body. On the 19th of March, about

3 o'clock in the morning, he was seized with a vomiting of blood. Though it soon stopped he grew noticeably weaker, showed every symptom of consumption, and constantly lost flesh and strength.

A few weeks later he was able to bear a drive in a closed carriage, and accompanied by his wife he removed to his brother James' house, it being large and in an airy part of town. I remained at his house, where I had been for some months on a visit, and took care of his children. He was still much bent on trying the effects of a sea voyage, and though his medical friends saw little to hope for, they did not wish to prevent the only chance he had of recovery. On the 4th of May, 1836, he embarked on board the Camden packet, Captain Tilly, for Falmouth, England, but everything was against him. The passage was much longer than usual with packets, the fare was miserable, and when my beloved child got to Falmouth he was quite exhausted, the fatigues and privations of the voyage having tended greatly to aggravate his disease.

After a short time, finding no hope of recovery, he anxiously wished to return by the next packet to Halifax, but the medical gentlemen gave it as their opinion that he could not survive the voyage, and he then gave up the idea, and calmly and patiently and full of the humble Christian's hope in Christ his Redeemer, and in His all-atoning blood, yielded with meekness to the will of his heavenly Father. He found much comfort from the kindness and Christian conversation of some truly pious persons, the Rev. Mr. Burchell of the Baptist Church at Falmouth, and a Mr. Bond of his church. They, their wives, and the doctor who attended him, soon forgot they had lately been strangers to him and felt and acted toward him as if he had been their brother. His deportment was sweet and amiable, calm and resigned, and all his mind was given to reading or hearing read the divine word of God. His wife and little Mary were with him, his two younger children having been sent to their grandmother Kelly's care at St. John, New Brunswick, previous to their parents leaving Halifax.

For a few days he rallied and his appetite was good, but his lungs were gone and he daily wasted away. He was sensible to the moment of his departure to his rest. He asked Mrs. Burchell what her brother the doctor said of the probabilities of his case. She answered with tenderness that he did not think he would live over two days. He appeared solemn and thoughtful, and after a little pause said he was resigned to the will of God. In his conversation he evinced a true faith in his Redeemer's blood and in the divine promises. The day before his death Mrs. Burchell said to him: "Mr. Johnston, do you know you will soon be entering the dark valley of the shadow of death; are you able to realize it?" He calmly and sweetly took up the verse and answered: "I will fear no evil, for thou art with me; thy rod and thy staff they comfort me." Such was the trust he had, and shall I doubt his happiness now? O no! may I be as well prepared as he was. He spoke a few minutes before his death, and took a teaspoonful or two of wine and water. When asked if it should be cold or warm, he said, "Warm." As soon as he was raised up and supported to swallow it, he shut his eyes and appeared to fall asleep. The doctor was on one side and his wife on the other, and as they laid him on his pillow, with one or two gentle breathings, he passed away.

Recollections of a Georgia Loyalist

"One gentle sigh, his fetters break,
We scarce can say he is gone."

My departed child was a truly religious man, pious and holy in his walk in life and deeply reverencing the sacred word of God. He died on the 11th of July, 1836, at Falmouth, England, and was interred in the Baptist burying ground there, far from all his beloved friends. His wife had a stone put over his grave, containing his name and age, with the simple inscription, " Blessed are the pure in heart, for they shall see God."

Mrs. Johnston, with little Mary, returned in the August packet to Halifax, and the meeting was a trying one to us all. As soon as she had recruited in some measure, with her child she set out for Annapolis on her way to St. John, where her two other children were with her mother and sisters. It was a great trial for her, meeting her fatherless babes. She remained there through the winter, her little boy being ill, and in the spring came with her children to Annapolis, some weeks after going with them to Wilmot, where she remained all summer and autumn. The country air restored James to health and greatly benefited them all. She now resides in Halifax, and it is a great comfort to us to have her here.

In March last, this year 1837, we were called to sustain another heavy affliction by the sudden death of our dear Amelia, the beloved wife of my son James and the tender and exemplary mother of his children. It was her delight to clothe the naked, feed the hungry, and educate poor little children who were growing up in poverty and vice. Not only was she concerned about people's secular needs, but she strove to impart religious knowledge to the minds of all she had the opportunity of conversing with. Her activity of mind and body in doing good was truly wonderful, and though she performed her outside charities so well, she did not forget her domestic duties nor ever neglect the minds and bodies of her own dear children, who numbered six. By her now bereaved and sorrowing husband (who sorrows, however, not without hope) is her loss deeply felt, for with her Christian conversation and her affectionate sympathy in his every care, sickness, or pain, she was the great solace of his life. Her death was a public loss; the poor of all descriptions mourned for her as their mother; even the Catholic priest, who knew her charities had been equally extended to his poor, lamenting her death, said to a friend of hers, " She was truly a good woman !" Thus mysterious are the ways of our heavenly Father. She was only thirty-five, and we looked for years of usefulness to be hers, but not so was her Lord's will; her work in His vineyard was done, and He perhaps foresaw evil to come and so in love and mercy called her early to Himself. May that blessed Saviour who took our nature upon Him, and who knows that we are weak and frail, be the support and comfort of her dear afflicted husband. The care of their six children devolves wholly upon him, and deeply does he feel the responsibility. Never was there a tenderer parent, nor one more deeply interested in his children's temporal and eternal welfare. Dear little Agnes, who had been delicate from her birth and about whom dear Amelia was very anxious, is his especial care. She was unwell for a time, but is now robust and hearty. Her sister Amelia, turned five years of age, is a fine, healthy child; his other daughter, in her sixteenth year, is a very promising girl and has an excellent disposition, and I hope by her docile and dutiful conduct will prove a great comfort to her beloved parent. I pray also that his three dear boys may be all he wishes. My prayers are daily offered at the throne of grace that they may be led to love and serve God and seek an abiding interest in Christ. My fixed home is with Lewis, and in my quiet apartment at his house I have the greatest possible freedom to read, write, and meditate.

．　．　．　．　．　．　．

At my time of life it is needful to cause the mind to dwell deeply upon the awful and momentous change which must soon take place in my frail body, and on the great transition of the soul. If prepared, what a delightful change from earth to heaven! If the prize is so great, what manner of persons ought we to be; how little ought we care for the perishing body so soon to be food for worms, and how exclusively ought we take thought for the soul that never dies.

LETTERS

DR. LEWIS JOHNSTON TO HIS SON WILLIAM MARTIN JOHNSTON

SAVANNAH, *July* 17, 1773.

DEAR BILLY:

We were all made very happy by receiving your letter of the 25th ult., together with the letters of Mr. Roberdeau and Dr. Rush. The very kind reception you met with from these gentlemen demands on our parts the warmest return of thanks, and on yours the most grateful acknowledgements, which will be best expressed by a constant care to please them, and to preserve that place in their regard and esteem which you have been so lucky thus early to obtain.

I cannot express the satisfaction it gave your mother and me when we read the handsome and friendly things they both said of you in their letters, and the great hopes they gave us of your success in your future studies. Your outset is fair and promising and let me beg of you earnestly for our sakes,

165

but more especially for your own, that such
agreeable prospects may not be blasted by any
want of application on your part, for however
good your opportunities of acquiring useful
knowledge may be, yet be assured that unless
you coöperate by unwearied diligence with
your teachers, all their pains will be but to
little purpose. It is my wish and intention
to give you such an education as may qualify
you for discharging the important duties of
the business you have made choice of, with
honour and reputation. A skilful physician
is one of the most respectable and useful persons in society; an ignorant pretender to it,
the most despicable and mischievous. I confess it is an arduous task to acquire that extensive knowledge which is necessary to qualify a man to make a figure in this profession,
but this so far from discouraging a young man
of spirit, ought rather to stimulate him in the
pursuit of it, as there is no branch of knowledge necessary for a physician which is not
agreeable and useful in itself, and what every
gentleman of liberal education ought at least
to have a general knowledge of. I intended
to have been more particular on this head,
and to have given you such advice as might

have been useful to you in regulating your conduct in other matters so as to avoid the errors that people at your time of life are in danger of falling into, but the situation of my mind renders me incapable of it, and 'tis with difficulty I have been able to throw together these general and unconnected observations. You may remember when you left us, your sister Nancy was sickly and had been so for some time. She continued in this way but daily losing flesh and strength, till the 14th instant, when it pleased God to deprive us of our sweet child. I need not tell you how great our affliction has been and still is, for you know how much we doated on her. May God make up to us this severe loss by doubling our comfort in those that are left. Your mother intended writing, but is not in a condition to do it now. She joins me, however, in praying for your happiness.

Your affectionate father,

Lewis Johnston.

SAVANNAH, *September* 6, 1773.

Dear Billy:

At the time I parted with you, though I thought it absolutely necessary for your own sake, yet I must confess I did it under very uneasy apprehensions, grounded on your want of application to your education, and to the violence of your temper, which though borne with by us would not fail when you went among strangers to create you enemies and be to you the source of much discomfort. Judge then, my son, how agreeably disappointed both your mother and I were when we receiv'd the first letters from your Guardians, full of your praises and of the great expectation they had of your turning out in a way that would do honour to you and us. I can truly say that this letter concerning you gave us more pleasure than you ever had given us from the hour of your birth. All your past errors were obliterated from our memories and you occupied the first place in our favour and affections. To dash all those pleasing hopes in the course of a few weeks, and fill our minds with the most pungent grief by your repeated acts of folly and indiscretion, was a cruelty to us that must cover you with shame and confusion, if you have any sense of humanity, not to say duty, remaining. My heart is so full on this occasion that I know not how to express my feelings. It is my duty so to represent your conduct that you may both see and feel the faults you have been guilty of, so as to be able to guard against committing the like in future. You solemnly declare you will not again give us cause of uneasiness; I am willing to believe it, but my dear son, do not for your own sake, for ours, trifle with me in this serious matter, for should you continue the like imprudences, the affections of your parents may be lost to you for ever, than which I cannot conceive a greater misfortune to a mind that is not totally deprav'd and divested of ev'ry feeling of humanity. God has pronounced a blessing upon the dutiful child and uttered a curse against the disobedient, which last never fails as far as my observation and experience reach (and I have known but too many fatal examples) to fall heavy upon the undutiful sooner or later. It is a matter of great consolation to me that I can with truth say I never gave one hour's uneasiness on account of my conduct to my father, to the hour of his death, though I was older when I had the heavy misfortune to lose him than you are now. I always had and still have the highest notions of the love and duty a child owes its parents, and I only wish my children to act on the same principles which I flatter myself guided me in my endeavours to discharge the duties I owed my parents.

Courage and spirit (as 'tis called) are no farther commendable qualities than while under the guidance of reason and religion, therefore avoid every occasion of disputes and quarrels, as they may, from the warmth of your temper, hurry you into some rash action that will make you miserable all the days of your life. I know of no cause that can justify a man either in risking his own life or in attempting to take another man's, except self-defence, the protection of an innocent person, or the safety of one's country. Such, I believe, are the real sentiments of every man of sense when he listens to the voice of reason and humanity, however differently he may act when he is influenced by false custom or the principles of a romantic honour. False custom, I say, for nothing can be truly honourable that is not strictly virtuous. Avoid carefully as your greatest bane, idle, disorderly, and vicious company. Many a young man of the best disposition and the greatest promise has been ruined by falling into that snare. Of this I hope you need no proof after what has happened to yourself; if you want more, look round and you will see but too many fatal examples. Did I think your errors arose from a want of knowledge of your duty I should enlarge much more on this subject, but as I know this is not the case, hinting at these things to you I hope will be sufficient, and it remains with yourself to profit by them or not. May God enable you to profit by them.

What now remains is to extricate you from the difficulties you have plunged yourself into; I have written fully to Mr. Roberdeau on the subject, and have directed him to use every method in his power to have the affair made up, but if that cannot be done, to send you immediately to New York to my friend, Dr. Peter Middleton, who is a professor in the medical college there and who will I doubt not receive you kindly. To conclude, let me once more earnestly intreat you to give close application to your studies, and make the best use of your time and opportunities, for if it should please God to call me out of this world soon (and you know my constitution does not promise long life) you must then return home where it will be impossible for you to get the education that is necessary. You do not want natural abilities, which if you take care to improve by a few years' study, will put it in your power to be happy all the remainder of your life. In full hopes of your endeavouring to make me happy, I am still, dear Billy,

Your affectionate father,

LEWIS JOHNSTON.

SAVANNAH, *Feby.* 5, 1774.

DEAR BILLY:

I rec'd your letters by the packet & was glad to hear you attended the classes closely. I wish I had also heard you gave application to your private studies, but I have already press'd these matters upon you with every argument and motion I thought would operate on one not totally void of reflection and generous sentiment. Should they fail of rousing you to a proper degree of attention, any thing else I might add would prove useless, and you may live to repent your conduct when it will be too late to remedy it. In such case the only consolation that will remain for me, as a recompense for the vast expense and care I have been at, is that I have done my duty. I am sorry to find Mr. Roberdeau & you continue on bad terms; he may be & I believe is too strict, but I cannot doubt of his good intentions. It gave me great concern to find you had left off attending Mr. Lind; you are deficient in the languages and your neglecting this opportunity can admit of no excuse. Dr. Rush recommends your attending Prince Town College in the spring. I hope you will make a better use of your time than you did last Summer. This step it seems is become necessary to break off some irregular connections, I am heartily sorry for it & hope it may have the desir'd effect, but remember that a change of place without a change of disposition will prove no remedy for the evil. I have written plainly to you on these matters; this my duty and a tender regard for your interest requires. 'Tis a disagreeable subject to me, pray let it be the last time I shall have occasion to enter on it. I intend sending your brother Andrew in April to Prince Town College, which I dare say will be very agreeable to you. He is a good and dutiful boy, & behaves so as to gain the esteem of all that know him. Give me grounds for indulging the pleasing hope of seeing you both return qualified to make a figure in your several stations; you both have good natural abilities.

Your mother has been dangerously ill. I need not tell you how tenderly anxious she is for your welfare.

I am yours,

LEWIS JOHNSTON.

SAVANNAH, *March* 13, 1774.

DEAR BILLY:

I wrote you a long letter by Capt. Bunner about the middle of last month which I hope you have receiv'd before now. The contents of it I earnestly recommend to your most serious consideration. This will be delivered to you by your friend Mr. John Habersham, to whom I refer you for the news of this place. I hope you will receive my next letter by your brother Andrew, whom I intend to send in Capt. Bunner's vessel the next voyage he makes from this. At the same time you may expect to see Mr. Read's son; I have recommended to his Father the sending him to Prince Town during the summer months. He is a sober young man,

174

very diligent in his application to his business & therefore a very proper companion for you. I hope to be able to send with Andrew a sufficient sum to keep you & him for one year in the prosecution of your studies; but whether I shall be able to do more for you I very much doubt as I dayly expect to be strip'd of every thing I am possessed of by my creditors, who are now determin'd to give me no longer indulgence. I mention this to you to show you the absolute necessity for your making the best use of your present opportunities, that you may not only be able to provide decently for yourself, but also be able to assist your brothers & sisters when it shall please God to render me incapable of doing it, or to take me from them. As I am convinced you do not want a proper degree of natural affection I hope this consideration will stimulate you to a diligent application to your business, as the only means by which you can have it in your power of being serviceable either to yourself or to them. At the time my father died he left a numerous family of small & helpless children. Tho' I was then younger than you are now I consider'd them as a charge which I was bound by every tie to protect & provide for to the utmost of my abilities, & I bless God for having given me hearty inclinations for the discharge of that duty, & for having put it in my power in some measure to supply the place of a husband to my worthy mother, & a father to my brothers & sisters. The consideration of my having conscientiously discharged that important duty fills my mind with such satisfaction & complacency as it is not in the power of fortune to deprive me of, & it will continue a source of rational pleasure to the last moments of my life.

I mention this, not out of ostentation, nor do I claim any merit for having done my duty in a case where if I had neglected it I must have been without natural affection & dead to every feeling of humanity. All I mean by this is to point out to my son the path I wish him to walk in should he ever be in like circumstances.

I have nothing further to add but my hearty prayers, in which your mother joins me, for your health & happiness. I am, dear Billy,

Your affectionate father,

LEWIS JOHNSTON.

Recollections of a Georgia Loyalist

My respectful compliments to Dr. Rush. I wrote to him by Capt. Bunner. You will if you have an opportunity, introduce Mr. Habersham to Dr. Rush as the son of a friend of mine.

SAVANNAH, *Decr.* 4, 1774.

DEAR BILLY:

I rec'd your letter of 13th ult. by the Georgia Packet, and one from my worthy friend Dr. Rush; the favourable account that gentleman gives us of your conduct affords the highest satisfaction to all your friends, and as they have the firmest reliance on your making it your study to merit the continuance of his approbation & friendship, all doubts & uneasiness on that head are utterly remov'd. I see by the Doctor's letter that you are attending the classes, which with the hospital will fully engage your whole time and not leave you a moment to spare for any other avocation. The very close application your studies will require may at first be a little irksome, but perseverance will soon render it easy and agreeable to you. It was my intention when you went to Philadelphia that you should spend two winters there and then go to Edinburgh, but on reflection I think it will be better for you to remain another winter in Philadelphia, and am happy to find Dr. Rush and I agree on this head. With respect to any objections you may have to Philadelphia, I think they cannot be of any great weight. You ought to consider that pleasure and amusement were not the things in view in sending you there; wherever you have the best chance of improvement is the place you should choose, independently of every other consideration. There is one point respecting your future conduct while you are absent from me which I have not yet touched on, but which I think it my duty now to mention, because you are come to that time of life when caution becomes necessary on this head, and because the want of this necessary caution and prudence had like to have prov'd fatal to me at the same period, being then unhappily depriv'd by death of the advice and admonitions of a tender father to guide me through the snares which surround unthinking youth. What I mean to warn you against are love entanglements, which are the more dangerous as they often wear the semblance of vir-

tue. As for the gross and animal gratifica-
tion of that passion which has assum'd the
name of love, I trust the delicacy of your own
sentiments will preserve you from it. Don't
mistake me, I am far from condemning a virtuous & well plac'd affection, I should be un-
grateful if I did, as it has prov'd a never
failing source of happiness to me and has
sweeten'd many a bitter portion in my life.
All I mean to warn you against is too early
connections of this kind, which as they are
generally more directed by passion than reason & prudence, are likely to become the
fatal sources of misery & affliction. A step
which in its consequences will infallibly
greatly affect the happiness or misery of a
man's whole life ought never to be taken
without the greatest caution. I hope I have
no reason to doubt your prudence on this
head; however, what I have said cannot be
improper. I have seen Mr. Le Conte & his
wife; she is an agreeable woman, and
speaks handsomely of you.

The Resolutions of the Congress I have
seen; they have much disappointed my expectations, for instead of endeavouring to draw
a line which ought to apportion the politi-

cal boundary between Great Britain and the Colonies, or of proposing a reasonable plan of accommodation, their general tendency to me seems to be to exasperate & inflame. I will not accuse them of any such intention, & I heartily pray I may be mistaken in the opinion I have form'd. There is to be another attempt made to bring this Province to accept the Resolutions; had they been framed with that prudence & moderation many expected, I believe they would have met with little opposition, but on the footing these matters now have I believe the best and wisest men will discountenance them.

I am yours affectionately,

LEWIS JOHNSTON.

FROM CAPT. WILLIAM MARTIN JOHNSTON TO HIS WIFE, AND FROM MRS. JOHNSTON TO HER HUSBAND.

SAVANNAH, *March* 3, 1780.

MY DEAREST HUSBAND:

I embrace this opportunity of writing by Capt. Murray, who goes for Ogeechee this day, and I hope may meet you there. I am very sorry you did not stay and go with him, as the passage round will be attended with many inconveniences, & be so tedious that a man of your impatient disposition must find it truly disagreeable.

You cannot conceive how much I regret the loss of your company; the state of mind that I was in when you left me, together with the thought of its being no longer a delusion but real, almost distracted me. Oh my dearest husband may you never experience the feelings of your Bess; the parting is but for a month, yet it appears a tedious, painful while to be separated from those we tenderly love. How shall I pass the lonely evenings, which when blessed with your presence I always considered so short. Last night when I went into my room and missed you, I thought my poor heart would have burst. I now find 'tis too tender, especially when I consider how subject it is to fresh troubles every day; but I will endeavour to bear things patiently. If you can only re-establish your health once more the hope of a speedy return will give pleasure to a heart weighed down with grief by your absence. May kind providence grant you a safe passage and every blessing this life can afford, is the fervent prayer of

Your affectionate wife,

ELIZA JOHNSTON.

SAVANNAH, *March* 10, 1780.

MY DEAREST HUSBAND:

I am this moment informed of an opportunity of writing by way of St. Augustine, which I eagerly embrace, well knowing by my own feelings the satisfaction you must receive at frequently hearing from me. I wish you had it in your power to write me constantly, but I hope after your arrival to hear very often, as communication is pretty frequent between the two provinces. Was I to write daily, the chief purport of my letters would be but to say I love you dearly and how happy hearing often from my dear, good husband would make his Bess.

I very often think that tho' fate has ordered it that we should be frequently separated she has yet left us a very great consolation in knowing that our hearts are united by the lasting bonds of love and friendship, which time nor absence can never in the least diminish. Oh, if we could never part, the meanest hovel in the world would satisfy my unambitious temper, but even that is a happiness we are denied, and all the pleasure I at present enjoy is to think how joyfully I shall meet you at your return. I hope that happy day is not far distant when I shall again behold my life, my husband, and be once more restored to his dear, fond arms. But the thought is so pleasing that I must plead an excuse for the strain in which it has led me, as you may think such rapturous expressions not so becoming in my sex. If you do, pray let the anxiety your absence creates serve as an excuse, together with the joy, the unspeakable joy, the thoughts of your return must occasion. The girls desire to be kindly remembered to you, I shall write papa by Mr. Schoide, and will request him to get our dear little Will for us.

Adieu my dearest husband, and may every blessing attend you, prays your affectionate wife, ELIZA JOHNSTON.

SAVANNAH, *March* 15, 1780.

MY DEAREST HUSBAND:

I wrote you a few days ago by the Commissary's Brig, but am not certain whether she has sailed yet, and fearing the contrary take this opportunity by Mr. Haven, who sets out for Ogeechee in the morning, as he expects the vessel has got round in which he goes from that place. I hope they may have a quick passage so that you may have the pleasure of hearing from me soon after your arrival. I give you no occasion to complain of my negligence, as I have written by every opportunity that has offered.

It made me very happy to hear of your having sailed, as I began to despair of your ever leaving Ogeechee; I hope ere this you are safely landed in St. Augustine.

If you can but return in good health once more to your Betsy I shall envy no creature breathing. Your presence always makes me happy beyond expression, and I have no wish but to please you in everything; if I but accomplish that, I shall be sufficiently happy. People here seem to be fond of following our example in the matrimonial way. Miss Tannatt was married the evening before last to Mr. Thomson, & our Sister has fixed the first Tuesday in April for her wedding day. Mrs. Muller will be married this week, so you see what a spirit of matrimony has got

ELIZABETH LICHTENSTEIN JOHNSTON
in later life

among them, but I dare venture to affirm none of them will be happier than ourselves. I even doubt their being as happy; the former is impossible. I must beg of you to get some sweetmeats done for me.

Adieu my dearest and best of husbands, may you be as happy as your absence from your Bess will admit of.

Your ELIZA JOHNSTON.

ST. AUGUSTINE, March 23, 1780.

MY DEAREST BETSEY:

I have just heard of a conveyance for Savannah, and the opportunity of writing affords me a pleasure which I have been a perfect stranger to since I left my lovely Betsey. I need not tell you how great my disappointment was in not having it in my power to write by a vessel that sailed the day after our arrival here. I was deprived of that great satisfaction by being unwell & not able to land till the day after. Our passage was tedious & disagreeable beyond expression.

I will say but little of St. Augustine as I am not in a mood to do it justice. 'Tis situated pleasantly and healthily, being quite open to the sea. I am very kindly received in all the families of any note here. They seem desirous to amuse and please me, yet I am neither well nor happy, in short a paradise would lose its beauties without my lovely Betsey.

> Dear Eliza, in some humble cell
> Could I but thee securely hold,
> In everlasting peace I'd dwell
> Nor think of power, nor covet gold
> The world no more I'd wish to see
> Content to dwell with love and thee.

Yours truly,
W. M. JOHNSTON.

ST. AUGUSTINE, *March* 27, 1780.

MY DEAR BETSEY:

A vessel has just arrived in two days from Savannah, and not one line for me. To what shall I impute this? My darling Betsey is not unwell I hope, and yet above all things I cannot impute it to neglect. My Betsey knows too well from her own feelings how great my disappointment must be.

I wrote a letter two days ago, which I expected to have sent by Mr. Findlayson, but was disappointed by his trip being put off. Nor do I know when I shall have an opportunity of sending this. However, I shall be ready for the first, and indeed I receive a secret pleasure from writing, which next to being with my Bess is the greatest of my life.

29.

I was just about closing my letter, very much dissatisfied indeed, when Mr. Haven surprised me with my dearest Betsey's two letters. The happiness they afford me is not to be expressed, and is to be felt but by few and I believe very few indeed. To taste this exquisite pleasure 'tis necessary to love as I do. And now my Betsey that I am pleased (and it is the first time I have been so since my arrival) let me think a little of my friends. I wish Miss Tannatt & Mrs. Muller much joy, but for my Sister Laleah, may she be happy as her own wishes can make her, or more ; may she be bless'd as I am. I am sent for to dinner, and the vessel sails this afternoon.

May God bless my dearest girl, prays your
W. M. J.

Recollections of a Georgia Loyalist

MY DEAR HUSBAND:

After a tedious passage of four days we arrived here late last night and found the family all in perfect health. Mrs. Farley is very unwell owing to the severe cold we had for a night and a day on board the boat.

An express going off this afternoon affords me this opportunity of writing my dearest husband, the only satisfaction I can have in the absence of the best of men, for I have no happiness but in your presence. The pleasure of meeting with friends I so dearly love was but momentary, for I cannot be cheerful when deprived of all I hold dear, and I fear my distress will be much augmented by the next account I receive from Charlestown, which I greatly apprehend will be of your having left that place in order to join your Regt. Let me beg you, my life, my husband, as you value the peace and happiness of your poor girl, not to think of doing so until you are perfectly restored to health. Try in the interim to get leave to come with papa, perhaps they will not refuse your request. Fortune has been favourable to me in one instance, in giving me a husband indulgent even to my foibles, whilst she has been cruel in obliging us to be separated. Would to heaven we were never to be parted and then my happiness would be complete and I should have no wish ungratified.

I shall take care to put your brother Lewis in mind of speaking to your father about getting you some employment in the civil line, may God hear my prayers and grant me success. I cannot express the feelings of my full heart to my best of men. I would tell you I love you more than my own life, but you are well convinced of that already, and I must beg and entreat that you will come by the first opportunity, if you possibly can consistently with duty.

May the All Wise Being protect & guard my dearest husband, is the ardent prayer of your faithful ELIZA JOHNSTON.

CHARLES TOWN, *Jany.* 2, 1781.

MY DEAREST BESS:

I have been looking for your letters with all the anxious expectation of one who fondly loves, till this morning the return of the boat that carried you to Savannah put an end to my hopes. I cannot account for this omission and am too much interested not to be hurt at it, indeed my whole happiness consists in hearing from you often, 'tis this alone which "heals each anxious care that love like mine in absence frames." I shall be under the necessity of joining the Reg't. soon, though I find the buying of horses will be very expensive and very difficult. Let me know as soon as possible whether I can get the horse I sent for. I do not believe our Reg't. will march with Lord Cornwallis; if it does not we shall be about Camden, and I look for the unspeakable happiness of seeing you in Savannah about the beginning of May. How heavy and unsupportable will the minutes be till then.

Adieu my darling Betsy,

W. M. J.

CHARLES TOWN, *Jan.* 3, 1781.

MY DEAR BESS:

I this day had the unspeakable satisfaction of receiving your letter. To know that you were well and with your friends has afforded me a pleasure to which I have been a stranger ever since our cruel separation. Yet I am not satisfied; in my Betsy's presence alone am I to expect happiness. I am surprised I did not get a letter from my father. It must be owing to his not knowing of the opportunity. I hope I may hear from him before I join the army. I have sent for horses and shall go for Camden as soon as the money for the Reg't. is drawn, which will be as soon as the Quartermaster-General comes to town. I wish it was possible for me to go to Savannah with propriety; it is not, however, and my Betsey I am convinced would not subject me to censure for any consideration whatever. Rest assured that as soon as possible I shall fly on the wings of love to all my happiness, my darling wife.

   Adieu.

     Your   W. M. J.

   CHARLES TOWN, *January* 9, 1781.

MY DEAR BETSEY:

I wrote you two letters last week, one by Capt. Cozens, who carried a bandbox which I hope you have received. One or two boats have arrived from Savannah without my hearing from you, which has been a great disappointment to me, for tho' 'tis but a few days since I received your letters I am anxious to hear from you again. To know that my Betsey is well is what only can afford me pleasure in her absence. Write very often, and particularly how you spend your time, who is most friendly and attentive to you, and I'll love them for their attention. Write that you are well but not very happy. Don't think me ungenerous, my Bess, when I tell you I would not be pleased to think you were perfectly happy in my absence, yet I am sure your happiness is dearer to me than my own life. This sentiment may appear strange to some, yet 'tis the language of love and my Betsey perfectly understands it. Remember me to my father and the girls. My father owes me two letters, and the girls a great many; they have not thanked me for the buckles yet, tho' I suppose you have taken the merit of that present to yourself. Your father will be in Savannah soon. Adieu.

Your   W. M. J.

SAVANNAH, *Jan.* 10, 1781.

MY DEAREST HUSBAND:

I rec'd yours of the 3d inst, which gave me a pleasure I have long been a stranger to. I have written you several letters since my arrival here & wish you may have rec'd them safe, tis the only satisfaction left us now, & that's but trifling when compared to the unspeakable anxiety our cruel separation occasions.

Oh my dear husband you cannot imagine the uneasiness your last letter gave me, where you mention intending soon to join the army. Why not give me one kind look before you go still farther; there certainly can be no impropriety in your being here for a few days. Indeed when I parted with you, you promised to accompany my father up, but I fear you then intended to deceive me. I do not wish you to act improperly, but my husband I'm no stoic. I cannot think of your joining the army without shuddering. The danger you will be constantly expos'd to is more than I can support, & I have not courage even to hope. I see no prospect just now of any thing worth your acceptance offering in the civil line, but I would be satisfied with a very little rather than live under such dreadful apprehensions for your safety. Your constitution will not bear the fatigue of a soldier's life, where you must always be exposed to the inclemency of the weather.

In short, while you continue in the army, wretchedness must be my portion. You promised me your picture in miniature, pray don't forget it, as you know not half the pleasure I shall receive, especially when deprived of the dear original. Were I to write volumes it would only be a repetition of how much I suffer by your absence, & how ardently I wish to see you. I entreat & beg you will be careful of your precious health, which is dearer to me than my own.

And now I must bid you farewell, & may every guardian angel attend & shield you from all dangers is the constant prayer of your distressed wife,

ELIZA JOHNSTON.

SAVANNAH, *Jan.* 16, 1781.

MY DEAREST HUSBAND:

An opportunity offers in the morning which I cannot fail of embracing, tho it is now very late & exceedingly cold. The pleasure I receive from writing my dearest husband is not to be expressed, and is only to be equalled by hearing often from you, a happiness I have but once experienced since I left Charlestown. This seems a little unaccountable when there have been four or five opportunities lately from thence. I would not for the world attribute your not writing to negligence, but would rather believe that you did not know of the chances. To suppose the former would make me wretched indeed, but the confidence I do and ever shall place in my dear, good man, removes every doubt on that head. I have a distant hope of seeing you soon, and expect to be agreeably surprised with a sight of you when I least expect it. I need not desire you to come as soon as possible, well knowing how equally anxious you are to see your fond, affectionate wife, whose whole happiness consists in your being with her. I wrote you the day before yesterday a long letter, indeed I never omit writing when opportunities offer. This goes by land in charge of Mr. Stork. I enclose you a watch paper, & beg you'll keep it for my sake. Do remember my advice to you in a former letter about gaming, tho I should hope you will not act contrary to my wishes in a matter so easily to be complyed with. Adieu.

Your   E. JOHNSTON.

Recollections of a Georgia Loyalist

MY DEAREST HUSBAND:

I wrote you twice this morning, I cannot say by whom as your brother forwarded them. You will receive this by Quan who goes to-morrow. I find so much pleasure & satisfaction in often writing my dearest husband that were it possible for opportunities to offer hourly I should not fail embracing them all. My father's stay with us is short, as he intends leaving this next Friday. The gentleman whom he came in quest of had left here a few nights before his arrival. Certainly he is a base wretch, & has given my father an immensity of trouble.

I have enclosed a memo. for a few articles which are not to be purchased here. You will pardon my troubling you with my trifling commissions; be assured nothing but necessity could induce me to ask a thing of you which really your sex have no business with. You'll probably think it encroaching beyond the privileges of a wife.

And I must intreat that you'll write me often, likewise your father, who is always happy to hear from you, tho' I am sorry to say he does not often enjoy that pleasure. He is exceedingly fond of your greyhound, as well as myself. She sleeps in the room with me every night, and when I awake I generally find her in bed with me. Send your picture by the first opportunity that offers, for I shall be very anxious until it arrives and much disappointed if 'tis not a strong resemblance. If it was the dear original I expected, with what pleasure would I anticipate our meeting. Can you not contrive, my dearest Love, to see your anxious Bess soon, as I have been some time from you? Surely there can be no impropriety in your paying me a short visit. Consider 'tis to see a wife who fondly doats on her husband, & whose constant and ardent prayers shall be daily offered up for his preservation and speedy return to the arms of her whose happiness alone consists in his dear presence.

Adieu, my Love.

Your   ELIZA JOHNSTON.

CHARLES TOWN, *Jany.* 18, 1781.

MY DEAR BESS:

I have written two Letters by your father, but his being detained a half hour longer affords me an opportunity of writing a few more lines to my dearest girl. I have sent you an Italian hound which is a great favourite of mine and therefore no trifling present. She has been witness to many a solitary hour I have spent since your absence, and by her fawning has seemed to sympathize in my anxiety. Save for me one of her handsomest pups.

Once more adieu, my beloved wife.

W. J.

January 24, 1781.

MY DEAREST LOVE:

Mr. Townshend this instant called to let me know he was going off immediately, an opportunity I could not fail of embracing, tho' I hardly have time for more than a few lines. A long letter, however, will be needless as I have already written you twice within these three days. I have only to request that you will be equally diligent in writing frequently, as 'tis the only pleasure I enjoy in your absence. You can have no conception how very insipidly time passes in your absence. The town is pretty gay just now but I have no relish for any amusement without my best of husbands. You know I am of a domestic disposition, and so have always preferred your society to all the amusements art could suggest. Happy should I esteem myself were I banished from the world and allowed no company but yours; the meanest hovel would satisfy my unambitious mind, and I cannot forbear accusing fortune of cruelty in having dealt her favours with a niggard hand.

Adieu, my ever dearest and best of men, may God for ever bless and protect you fervently prays your

ELIZA JOHNSTON.

Poor Mr. Wyley died yesterday after a painful illness.

SAVANNAH, *April* 23, 1781.

MY DEAR WILLIAM:

It is with pleasure I inform you that Mr. Wylly called this morning to acquaint your Father that the troop of horse so long spoken of is now actually to be raised for the defence of this Province, but the latter does not think it worth your acceptance as the pay is only ten shillings per day. Mr. Wylly intends writing you on the subject, and I think you may get it if you choose to apply.

I am convinced your feelings in the matter

199

are similar to mine, and doubt not of your accepting a thing that may enable us to live together, as my present life is wretched indeed. Not even my infant's smiles can compensate to me for your absence. I have long been expecting my father, and I wonder at his stay. I hope for a large pacquet by him. And, my dear, let me remind you of the promise you have made me not to enter again into that dreadful vice, gaming. Consider the difficulties it had nearly involved you in and shudder. Oh think of my happiness, think of your child who claims your support, and for his sake do not persist in what may end in your total ruin. Your father will also write you. Adieu my love.

Your affectionate wife,

ELIZA JOHNSTON.

CHARLES TOWN, *April* 23, 1781.

MY BESS:

Your dear letter (which I this minute received) gives me a pleasure which I have been for some time unacquainted with, and I almost forget the cruel feelings which our separation must ever create. Yes, my dear girl, I would with pleasure accept of what you wish and mention, for a bare sufficiency with you would to me be more luxurious than the splendor of a crown without you. I have written Mr. Wylly particularly. Your father has been detained by business, but sets out in about a week for Savannah. I am afraid I shall lose this opportunity.

Adieu my love.

W. M. J.

CHARLES TOWN, *April* 24, 1781.

MY DEAR BESS:

I arrived here after a pleasant passage of three days. I am tolerably well, but how shall I express the anxiety that has disturbed my heart ever since I left all that's most dear to me. A thousand feelings which till now I have been a stranger to fill me with fears hardly to be borne. What would I at this moment not give to behold my darling wife and lovely babe, but this is a pleasure I must long be unacquainted with, and the pain which this cruel separation must always create can only be alleviated by often hearing from my dearest Betsey. I shall send as many of the things you want as I can recollect, by your father, who goes in a few days, but I have lost the memorandum. The picture which you will receive is thought to be a very good likeness. You will also receive a locket, on one side your mother's hair & on the other side mine. If you do not want the locket you now have, enclose it to me in your next with a lock of your hair & some of my dear boy's. I do not think I shall leave town before Qua returns. Send the two bedsteads & Juno by him. Adieu, my dearest Bess, give my sweet little fellow a thousand kisses for me. Your W. M. J.

CHARLES TOWN, *April* 29, 1781.

MY DEAR BESS:

I but this minute heard of Mr. Tattnal's going for Savannah, and with pleasure embrace the opportunity of writing you a few lines. I cannot tell you how anxious I am to hear that you & my dear little boy are well. Mr. T. will deliver your three fans, which you will dispose of as you please; they were all I could get just now, but by your father I will send one of a different fashion for yourself, and one of the same kind as these, which I suppose will fall to Laleah's lot. You'll also receive a handsome coral for my sweet little fellow, though I am sure it cannot add to his loveliness. I wrote you a letter by Qua, which I am in doubts of your receiving, as 'tis said he is taken. It is uncertain when I shall be able to join the Regt. as Camden is close besieged by Greene's army. Lord Cornwallis has marched from Wilmington, I suppose for the relief of Camden, tho' we are not in the least apprehensive but Lord Rawdon can of himself defend the place. Greene made two attacks on a mill adjacent to Camden and on which our troops chiefly depend for provisions, in both of which he was repulsed. The latter part of this letter is intended for my father. I would have written him, but Mr. T. waits for this.

Adieu, my darling Bess. I am well but cannot be happy while absent from you.

W. M. J.

CHARLES TOWN, May 11, 1781.

MY DEAR BESS:

Your two letters by Mr. Charlton this moment came to hand. I need not say how happy they made me. I have counted every tedious moment as it pass'd since I last heard from you. I should have left town yesterday but my anxiety to hear from you and some little business induced me to ask leave for a few days indulgence in town. I am in treaty about the sale of my company with an officer of the 60th Regt., tho' I fear he will not be able to make it worth my while, unless I were sure of something in Savannah. I will be more particular in my next.

May God ever bless my Betsy.

W. JOHNSTON.

May 25, 1781.

MY DEAREST HUSBAND:

I embrace this opportunity by Qua of writing a few lines to my dearest and best of men, whose greatest satisfaction I am sensible of is hearing from his Bess. And it shall be my endeavour to increase as much as possible the happiness of a husband who is dearer to me than life. I am anxiously expecting my father, and hope for an immense pacquet. Write frequently, let me only hear that you are well and I will be satisfied, for you know not to what an excess I doat on my generous, kind William. You are the idol of my fond & constant heart, and in you I can repose every anxious thought. Perhaps we may yet

204

enjoy the sweets of domestic life & be freed
from the cares & disquietudes which a soldier's life creates; would that happy day were
arrived.   One thing I take the liberty of
hinting, as 'tis to our mutual advantage.
You must know, my dear husband, your pro-
pensity to play; 'tis a great misfortune, especially as your family are increasing; but as I
flatter myself you upon reflection detest it
as much as myself, 'tis my earnest prayer and
entreaty that you will guard against a vice so
destructive and ruinous in its nature.   In
your last, you regret not being deserving of
me; I fear that sentence took its rise from
your having broke through the solemn promise you made me of never risking your interest and my happiness at the gaming table
again.

Your son is better.   He is a handsome,
sweet fellow, only he has receiv'd a rather
large proportion of your passionate temper.
I have at last got your picture, 'tis thought a
good likeness, but for my part I cannot think
you have had justice done you.   The painter
has given it a sour look, and made the com-
plexion much darker than yours; in short I
want the dear original.   My father has re-

fused the troop, the service being too fatiguing. The rebels encroach fast upon us, and have been within five miles of the town. I am very drowsy and must wish you a good night.

Adieu, my dearest Love.

Yours truly,

ELIZA JOHNSTON.

SAVANNAH, *September* 20, 1781.

MY DEAREST W. :

I eagerly embrace the opportunity by Mr. McPherson of entreating you to come to town before you march; if you can with propriety, pray oblige me. My dearest of men you know not how very anxious I am to see you. Pray don't think of moving whilst a superior force of the enemy are so nigh. Prudence is as necessary a requisite as true courage, and as you have ever given proof of the latter no one will doubt your having it. Myself and child are well, come and see the sweet boy, and don't miss such frequent opportunities of writing as you have hitherto done. Your affectionate

E. JOHNSTON.

Recollections of a Georgia Loyalist

MY DEAR HUSBAND:

I received your dear and welcome letter this afternoon by Mr. McPherson. I cannot express to you my feelings when I heard of your being safe. I could only give it vent by pouring forth my thanks to my Maker for preserving the husband and father. I think we can never be sufficiently thankful; had it not been for the interposition of Providence what a wretch should I this night have been, alas, an afflicted widow with a helpless orphan. I cannot be easy until I see you, my beloved husband. I must be anxious, but I hope that happiness will not long be denied me. My Andrew is well, and a fine lovely boy he is. Give my love and duty to my father, let him know the vessel has not yet arrived with his things. And may the Almighty continue to protect & bless you both is the fervent prayer of your

E. JOHNSTON.

CHARLESTOWN, *August* 15, 1782.

MY DEAR HUSBAND:

I rec'd yours, and am happy to inform you that Andrew is no worse, tho' I see no material alteration for the better. I rode out yesterday with him, and mean to do so while I can. I still keep well, and have no reason to expect being otherwise for this week to come. Let me beg to see you to-morrow or the day after. 'Tis cruel not to visit me often, especially when 'tis through your means the Regiment are kept on the Island in preference to Charlestown. I must compare you to the old Romans in ancient times, who were so disinterested as to sacrifice wives & children and every other consideration for the welfare of their country. Do, my Regulus, be less rigid, and come before the anxiously expected yet dreaded hour arrives. I am told of a vessel being sighted, and it is reported, a fleet of thirteen sail, which I believe is uncertain. Send some butter and melons. Remember I look for you to-morrow.

Adieu.

E. Johnston.

St. Augustine, January 3, 1783.

My dear Husband:

I arrived here a few days ago after a tedious passage of three weeks. We were detained a week off St. John's, waiting for a convoy round, and were obliged to come without at last, as the anchoring off that bar was by no means safe.

I found all your family well but much dissatisfied with their situation. It is a dreadful winter country, constantly wet or cloudy. I have not seen a fair day since my arrival. I repent sincerely of not going with you to New York, as I doubt not of your doing by this time. I wish it may answer for the best, tho' it will cost me many months uneasiness until we meet. I expect to join you in the spring, if you do not arrive here in the interim.

I cannot advise with regard to your future prospects in life; at present they appear in a most unfavourable light. At the same time I am very anxious for your settling soon, to enable us living together, for what is life when separated from my kind William? Indeed, my love, my heart overflows with gratitude when I reflect how happily my lot has fallen to get so good and kind a husband. My Andrew has been unwell since our arrival, but is much recovered. As for Kate, she is a sweet, healthy girl and very pretty.

Recollections of a Georgia Loyalist

Out of the last fleet from Charlestown there have been sixteen sail of small vessels lost on and about the Bar. There are six or eight high on the beach. One of these had the greatest part of Dr. Baron's property on board, and I much fear he will be a great sufferer. 'Tis amazing how such a place was ever settled. Will you send me your picture in miniature? If it is a good likeness, I shall prize it highly. Embrace every opportunity of writing, and take care of your precious health; don't think of entering into the cavalry. Remember me to Mrs. Thomas, and Miss Hatch and her sister.

Adieu, may heaven bless my dearest Love fervently prays Your

E. JOHNSTON.

ST. AUGUSTINE, *April* 20, 1783.

MY DEAREST LOVE:

I have already written you a few lines by this opportunity. I flatter myself I shall now see you very soon, and I hope to have my expectations confirmed by the return of Dr. Fraser's schooner, which is expected immediately. I was determined to sail, the first good chance that offered, for New York,

Recollections of a Georgia Loyalist

had not a packet arrived from London with the accounts of a peace being made, with terms most shameful to Britain. The war never occasioned half the distress which this peace has done, to the unfortunate Loyalists. No other provision has been made than just recommending them to the clemency of Congress, which is in fact casting them off altogether. We have had no accounts from Georgia since they received word of the peace, but we fear their prosperity will not tend to moderate them.

Should your Regiment be ordered to Canada or Nova Scotia I beg you will send for me, unless you should get leave of absence. I wish you here chiefly on your father's account, who is unwell both in body and mind as he lets this news of a peace prey too much on his spirits. But how can it be avoided with such a family and such prospects—'tis enough to distract him. My children are well—Andrew is a great prattler and Kate thrives finely. She is a sprightly, good-natured slut, with a pair of lovely blue eyes. You have my measure for shoes, which article I am much in need of. Be careful of your cash & buy nothing else for me, I must give up finery altogether now, but that will be no sacrifice to me.

> Adieu my Love.
> Yours truly,
> ELIZA JOHNSTON.

ST. AUGUSTINE, *October* 11, 1783.

MY DEAREST WILLIAM:

I wrote you a few days ago by Mr. Peterson, who goes to Halifax and has promised to forward my letter immediately from thence. The Almighty send you safe and speedily to Edinburgh, where you will embrace (I hope) every opportunity of improving and making yourself useful in your profession. Oh my husband, was it not for the pleasing hope that a short time will render us independent of your good father (whom I have long been a burthen on) I could not at all support your absence.

Sometimes my extreme tenderness and anxiety for you make me anticipate the greatest evils; you know I ever had a strong bent that way. The thought of the coast of England in the winter season terrifies me. You that are my only refuge and hope, can I be too anxious for your safety, my best, my

212

only friend? Would but my father be generous and kind, and send for me, your half pay (which I must at any rate draw in America) would support myself and children very well in England with him, and I should have a happiness to which I am now a stranger. My whole time is spent in my own room, and I find my love of solitude hourly increases. 'Tis pleasing to indulge melancholy when it is occasioned by the absence of those we fondly love. A thousand tender scenes arise in my memory, which please and pain by turns my afflicted heart, but never can I forget the agonies which rent my heart that morning which deprived me of my dearest of men. When I wish my tears to flow in torrents, then I paint our cruel separation in its most horrid colours. To increase my wretchedness, my darling girl does not recover her strength or flesh, tho' she has cut most of her teeth, which was the cause of her illness. My boy is quite well and so engaging, he moves my heart with his fond endearments, which he was always so lavish in bestowing on his happy father. The evening before you left us how fondly did he cling about you, as if he had a presentiment of the loss he was to sustain for a long time; but I pain your parental breast too severely by recalling scenes which are not to be recalled to memory without the most poignant grief.

If I could only hear of your safe arrival my mind would be much easier, I must therefore wait patiently for that event.

We have accounts in town that the Floridas are to be held, but 'tis not generally credited. The troops embarked yesterday for Halifax, and those that chose to remain were disbanded a week ago. All is very quiet as yet; the militia turn out with great alacrity and I hope nothing disagreeable will happen.

We had a dreadful gale of wind a few days ago, which caused a general alarm, as the tide rose above Payne's corner. I wish I were safe from the country. I hope soon to hear from my loved William, who I must beg will write long and tender letters. Be circumstantial in all the little incidents that occur to you, it will amuse me. You will, I am sure, be a great economist, and you need send me nothing but a few magazines. Mrs. Catherwood is very polite and friendly. I have had several books from her which I was at a loss to procure and I find reading an excellent amusement when I am inclined to be melancholy.

I know not how to quit my pen and very frequently forget and suppose myself in conversation with you, tho' I should not forget the hint once given me that my letters were lengthened beyond my good sense in general. Capt. Randall will take charge of this. And now I bid adieu to my ever dearest of men; may every blessing attend you for your kindest care and attention to your once truly happy, tho' now afflicted wife,

ELIZA JOHNSTON.

ST. AUGUSTINE, *January* 2, 1784.

MY DEAR WILLIAM:

I am happy that an opportunity offers of writing my best beloved, whose arrival I am now extremely anxious to hear of, especially as you sailed in a boisterous season of the year; but God I hope has through His infinite mercy preserved a life far dearer than my own. Your father has rec'd many applications from Charleston for the purchase of his negroes, & the best security in that country is offered, but he wishes the interest to be secured in England, which I fear will not be in their power. He has written the terms, and is now in expectation of a final answer. I have a presentiment that the answers will agree with my wishes. Seven transports have arrived at St. Mary's from New York, for the use of the Loyalists. It will be a great expense saved, your father having his family transported passage free. Every person seems anxious for the packet's arrival, which has been long expected. I wish she may have been detained, as I may thus hope to hear of your arrival, news which will amply compensate me for the uneasiness her stay in general occasions.

I meant to write you by Col. Deveaux, who promised to call for my letter, but his carrying off a Miss Warner obliged him to make a precipitate retreat. This place is extremely dull for want of arrivals from England, I almost wish for the Spaniards, to cause a little bustle. My children (thanks to that All Merciful Being who preserved them) are both well. We can never be sufficiently thankful for the miraculous recovery of our beloved girl, who is now quite well and just begins to step alone. Andrew is grown remarkably fat and often speaks of you.

Recollections of a Georgia Loyalist

Mr. Baillie leaves town this evening, who is to have charge of this. Another opportunity will offer in about a month, when I hope to write more fully and of a certainty what our route will be. I hope you have seen my dear parent, how happy should I feel myself in meeting him once more. A ship has just appeared, I hope 'tis the long expected packet. Could I but have a few lines from my dear William what a happiness would it be to your Bess. My children kiss you through me. Adieu my best of men. May every angel guard and protect your precious life, and oh may we shortly meet, never more to part in this life. Once more adieu, my darling husband.

Your ELIZA JOHNSTON.

N. B. We have just heard from the ship, which to our disappointment is not the packet but a transport from New York. She is one of eight that sailed for St. Mary's.

St. AUGUSTINE, January 15, 1784.

MY DEAREST HUSBAND:

Yesterday I had the unspeakable pleasure of receiving yours by the brig Caroline. It was doubly satisfactory as I was anxious to hear of your safe arrival, you having sailed in a bad season of the year. Let me pour forth my gratitude and thanks to my Creator for the preservation of my husband and the happy recovery of my darling daughter. Andrew is quite well. I am somewhat surprised at your expecting such an infant should know his letters, who is not three years old yet, and think it full time a twelvemonth hence to begin him. Many sensible people will tell you 'tis not right to stuff a child with learning before his mind has had time to expand.

I suppose your short arrival in the city prevented your writing more fully. I wished much to hear whether you were better of that cruel disorder which distressed you so much when here. I am not just now in any particular want of money, and as your father is still in suspense what his next move will be I shall not draw for any until we are better settled. Probably if your father disposes of his negroes he may go to Scotland, tho' I have my fears on that head, as from the flattering accounts the Loyalists there give of their large crops of indigo he seems to have an idea of Jamaica. I should be distressed

218

to take my children to so very unhealthy a place.

Your father is greatly surprised at your remaining in London, as your studies might be prosecuted with more success in Edinburgh, and I fear he thinks your reasons not the best for determining as you have done. I cannot write my father at present, but an opportunity will offer shortly by which I shall write him. I am surprised he did not send the children toys as he promised them; as for myself I want nothing. In your absence dress has no charms for me. I have neither spirits nor inclination to take part in any amusements.

I have rec'd all the attention from your family that I could possibly wish for, Mrs. Wood not excepted, who has paid me more attention than I had reason to expect after the cruel manner in which you behaved to her. I am yours truly,

ELIZA JOHNSTON.

ST. AUGUSTINE, *Feby.* 3, 1784.

MY DEAR HUSBAND:

I have just rec'd yours of the 17th November. Words cannot express my feelings upon hearing of your illness. To think my William should have been in danger and not one tender friend to administer comfort and pay that attention which is both pleasing and necessary to a sick person. You wrote a letter to your father during your illness, which I was kept ignorant of. I have this instant rec'd another letter of 6th December, which says not a word of your precious health.

I wish you had been more particular on that head, as the good health of you and my children is the greatest satisfaction I can have. How much am I obliged to you, my dearest Love, for granting me leave to accompany your father if I please, which, be assured, I do most readily. If he determines on going to England you may depend on seeing me. I have written you repeatedly since you left me and cannot suppose you think your Bess inattentive, whose gratitude as well as tenderest love would induce her to write you by every opportunity. Therefore dispel every melancholy idea, and hope in the spring to be blest with your wife and dear infants. Your brother Lewis has written you of the sad accident which Andrew met with by a fall from a balcony. His thigh bone was snapped in the middle, but it happily was not splintered and he is now perfectly recovered. 'Tis amazing with what patience he bore the pain and confinement attending it. My Kate is perfectly well & runs alone but is the greatest vixen in Florida. I am uneasy at not hearing from my father, but as you did not mention him think still there must be a letter somewhere for me.

This has been a day of sad confusion and has occasioned many long faces, as the people here were quite sanguine in the expectation of the two Floridas being held. The arrival of a packet, however, has dashed their hopes and made their disappointment unspeakable. Your father remains still at a loss what to determine with regard to his next movement, he not having rec'd answers from Charleston with respect to the sale of his negroes. I must bid you adieu, with my earnest prayers for your future health and safety, which God Almighty preserve. Yours,

ELIZA JOHNSTON.

Recollections of a Georgia Loyalist

My dearest Husband:

I have written you repeatedly lately, but must not omit a few lines more to congratulate you on the happy prospect we have of meeting early in the summer. I cannot describe my feelings but I am all impatience to be gone, and I hope by the middle of April we shall sail from St. Mary's. The transports that we expect from England are not arrived, but I hope for a large pacquet by them. You have disappointed me greatly in the letter way, yours being shorter and less particular than I could have wished. Every trifle that concerns my William would give me pleasure. Your father has disposed of your negroes for four hundred & fifty pounds, Colonel Brown was the purchaser. I kept Hagar as a nurse for the expected stranger, who I hope will shortly make its appearance. I anticipate your feelings when kissing the lovely infants, for I hope my little expected will live to bless his anxious mother with a smile. Your sister Laleah accompanies your father to Scotland, being in a bad state of health, but I hope the change of climate will

222

be productive of every good she can wish, for she is a most amiable woman. It will much embitter the happiness I look for in meeting with my husband should you not receive her with that tender affection which she is deserving of. Mrs. W. declares herself ignorant of the cause of your displeasure, nor indeed can I give a reason strong enough to induce you so to lay aside all brotherly affection as never once to mention her in your letters; it hurts me severely. I did not suspect you of so unfeeling a heart as you have shown on this occasion. For my sake then, meet all your friends as if nothing disagreeable had ever passed, and be assured should you refuse this request I never will forgive your cruelty. If you had seen your sister Mrs. W.'s distress when your son met with that accident, and her attention to him, I am confident you would blush to think how ill you have treated her. I hope I need say no more on this subject in future. Adieu.

Your tenderly affectionate

ELIZA JOHNSTON.

Recollections of a Georgia Loyalist

MY DEAREST HUSBAND:

'Tis impossible, wholly impossible, to convey an idea of the joy I feel at being safely anchored in this port, but I feel a damp on my spirits in anticipating your sufferings and your anxiety on our account, occasioned by our arriving later than you had reason to expect from the letters you no doubt received. We did not leave St. Mary's until the 30th of May, and we were in the Cove of Cork a week. We shall remain here some days until Doctor Johnston goes to Glasgow and procures us lodgings there for a short time. I shall experience many anxious moments until I hear from my dear husband. Oh may an All Gracious Providence have preserved my tenderest and best of men for a happy meeting once more with his anxious wife.

Mrs. Wood has accompanyed us and is ready to lie in. Remember my request in a former letter, and let her not, I beseech you, be shocked in her present situation by any unkind behaviour of yours, but meet her, my Love, as if nothing had passed. The children are well. Adieu my Love.

Your ELIZA JOHNSTON.